Mechanical Imagery in Spanish Golden Age Poetry

José Porrúa Turanzas, S.A.
EDICIONES

stuöia humanitatis

Directed by
BRUNO M. DAMIANI
The Catholic University of America

ADVISORY BOARD

Mechanical Imagery

In Spanish Golden Age Poetry

Daniel L. Heiple

Publisher and distributor
    José Porrúa Turanzas, S.A.
    Cea Bermúdez, 10 - Madrid-3
    España

Distributor for U.S.A.
    Studia Humanitatis
    1383 Kersey Lane
    Potomac, Maryland 20854

Printed in the United States of America
Impreso en Los Estados Unidos

Cea Bermúdez, 10 - Madrid-3
Ediciones José Porrúa Turanzas, S.A.

Table of Contents

Preface   vii

PART I.   Poetry and Science in the Golden Age

   1.   The Scientific Revolution in Spanish Poetry 1

   2.   The Baroque Image   15

   3.   Metaphysical Poetry in Spain   33

PART II.   Technical Instruments

   4.   The Balance Scale   51

   5.   The Geometer's Compass   67

   6.   The Mariner's Compass   87

PART III.   Time and the Measurement of Time

   7.   Concepts of Time in Pastoral Poetry   109

   8.   The Sundial and the Hourglass   127

        The Sundial   131
        The Hourglass   140

9. The Mechanical Clock   149

    The Allegorical Clock   153
    Time and the Lover's Anxiety   162
    The Clock as Moral Emblem   168

Conclusion   179

Preface

The seventeenth century, the age of the scientific revolution, also saw the appearance of mechanical and scientific imagery in poetry. This imagery usually does not involve complex scientific notions, but most often consists of simple tools and devices used as analogies for abstract concepts. Since this imagery is considered to be an important aspect of metaphysical poetry, the first three chapters explore the attitudes towards science in Spain, the structure of Baroque imagery, and the nature of the metaphysical style. The following chapters study the appearance of specific images in seventeenth-century Spanish poetry. Since each device relies on traditional associations and scientific knowledge, the study includes background for understanding its context. The balance scale is related to justice and salvation; the draftman's compass recalls the idea of the circle as the most perfect of geometrical forms; the navigational compass relies on a field of scientific theory; and the timepieces, the sundial, hourglass and mechanical clock, involve concepts of time which are studied fully in a separate chapter.

Rather than extract a few lines from many poems, the present study, wherever feasible, presents an explication of the complete poem. Even though this practice may at times introduce less relevant material and result in a diffuse discussion, it has the advantage of regarding each image in its full context. The critical approach that studies fragments of poems to demonstrate a point often overlooks significant aspects of the poetry by ignoring the context of the ideas.

Spanish criticism has generally avoided the study of metaphysical poetry, partly because the metaphysical movement did not flourish in Spain to the extent that it did in England. Spanish taste for elegance was incompatible with the harsh realities faced by the thought-provoking metaphysical poets, and Spanish poetry tended to avoid commonplace vocabulary, one of the important building blocks of metaphysical poetry in England. With the revival of Donne and Góngora in the present century, English criticism has tended to focus on the study of metaphysical poetry and Spanish critics have concentrated on the High Baroque[1] or *culterano* style of Góngora.

The importance of the metaphysical mode in Spain has mainly been noted by scholars in comparative literature. Arthur Terry used the concept of metaphysical to analyze Quevedo's conceits, and Emilia Kelley applied the fruits of a half century of English critical investigation of metaphysical poetry to the study of Quevedo.[2] Warnke's anthology of metaphysical poetry included poems by San Juan de la Cruz, Lope de Vega, Quevedo, and Sor Juana Inés de la Cruz.[3] In a study on Baroque poetry, Cohen included a poem by the Mexican Sandoval y Zapata, lamenting that such a fine poet has been completely ignored.[4]

---

[1] This term comes from Frank J. Warnke, *Versions of Baroque* (New Haven: Yale University Press, 1972), 12.

[2] Arthur Terry, "Quevedo and the Metaphysical Conceit," *BHS* 35 (1958), 211-222, and Emilia Navarro de Kelley, *La poesía metafísica de Quevedo* (Madrid: Ediciones Guadarrama, 1973).

[3] Frank J. Warnke, *European Metaphysical Poetry* (New Haven: Yale University Press, 1974).

[4] J. M. Cohen, *The Baroque Lyric* (London: Hutchinson University Library, 1963).

Mechanical and scientific imagery is an important aspect of metaphysical poetry. Dr. Johnson, whose essay on Cowley brought into prominence, albeit in a derogatory sense, the term "metaphysical," was the first critic to observe the importance of learning in metaphysical poetry.[5] Because the poets' main interest was poetry—not science—, their learning could be drawn rather indiscriminately from the pseudo-sciences, from the scholastic philosophers, and at times from the new advances of the scientific revolution. This uncritical mixture of pseudo-scientific notions and learning made the derogatory term "metaphysical" attractive to Dr. Johnson.

While most uses of mechanical and scientific imagery in poetry, both English and Spanish, cannot be classified as purely scientific, its presence in poetry forms a significant departure from the limiting canon of sixteenth-century Petrarchan imagery. The present work studies the importance of mechanical and scientific imagery in Spanish seventeenth-century poetry, and it is hoped that it will provide a significant step towards the recognition and appreciation of the Spanish metaphysical school.

---

[5] Samuel Johnson, *Lives of the English Poets,* ed. George Birbeck Hill (Oxford, 1905; rpt. New York: Octagon Books, 1967) I, 19, 23. In a forthcoming article in *Comparative Literature*, I discuss the meaning of "metaphysical" in the seventeenth century.

I would like to thank my friends who helped me with this book: Tom Montgomery and Mario Ullivarri who listened and commented on every step of production; Alexander Parker who introduced me to this material; my parents Robert and Violet Heiple for their moral support; Marina Kaplan and George Cummins for help with basic concepts; Dan Balderston for carefully reading the manuscript; John Nitti for advice on printing; Bruno Damiani for excellent suggestions on preparing the manuscript for publication; and others who offered help at the last moment.

PART I

Science and Poetry
in the Spanish Golden Age

1. The Scientific Revolution
in Spanish Poetry

This study examines in depth a major innovation in seventeenth-century Spanish literature: the introduction of mechanical and geometrical imagery into poetry. Such imagery is practically non-existent in sixteenth-century writers, most of whom never employ images of devices, machines or geometrical layout of space. While this imagery is not abundant in seventeenth-century writers, its appearance signals a new trend that is of capital importance in the study of seventeenth-century thought and letters.

The existence of a copious critical literature in English treating the relationship between science and poetry contrasts sharply with the paucity of similar studies for Spanish poetry.[1] The Spaniards' traditional

---

[1]   Outstanding among the English studies are those of Douglas Bush, *Science and English Poetry* (New York: Oxford University Press, 1950); Hedley Howell Rhys, *Seventeenth Century Science and Arts* (Princeton: Princeton University Press, 1961); Alan G. R. Smith, "Science and Literature," in *Science and Society in the Sixteenth and Seventeenth Centuries* (New York: Harcourt, Brace, Jovanovich, 1972), 157-172; Joseph Anthony Mazzeo, "The Idea of Progress: Science and Poetry," in *Renaissance and Revolution* (New York: Pantheon Books, 1965), 336; Marjorie Hope Nicolson, *The Breaking of the Circle* (New York: Columbia University Press, 1965); and

adversity to science and the scarcity of scientific references in their poetry provide grounds for concluding that the study of science and poetry in Spain is not a viable topic. The scientific revolution of the seventeenth century was primarily a northern European movement which did not reach Spain until the eighteenth century, and then only sporadically. Poetry anthologies show that mechanical and scientific imagery is extremely rare, confirming the view that science was not important in Spanish Golden Age thought. A number of poets never employed this type of imagery, and even those who did, used it infrequently.

In spite of its limited extension, the appearance of mechanical imagery in Spanish poetry is highly significant, for this imagery has often been considered an essential element in metaphysical poetry. Donne's image in *A Valediction, Forbidding Mourning* comparing two lovers to the legs of a compass is a prime example of metaphysical wit:

> If they be two, they are two so
> As stiffe twin compasses are two,
> Thy soule the fixt foote, makes no show
> To move, but doth, if the'other doe.

> And though it in the center sit,
> Yet when the other far doth rome,
> It leanes, and hearkens after it,
> And grows erect, as that comes home.

Allen G. Debus, *Man and Nature in the Renaissance* (Cambridge, England: Cambridge University Press, 1978). The studies by F. Picatoste, *Calderón ante la ciencia* (Madrid: 1881) and J. Grinda y Forner, *Las ciencias positivas en Calderón de la Barca* (Madrid: M. P. Montoya y Compañía, 1881) cannot really compare with the above studies. Elias Rivers, "Nature, Art and Science in Spanish Poetry of the Renaissance," *BHS,* 34 (1967), pp. 266-55, examines nature and science in the pastoral and Sor Juana Inés de la Cruz's ambivalence towards science and man's ability to understand natural forces.

> Such wilt thou be to mee, who must
> > Like the other foot, obliquely runne;
> Thy firmnes makes my circle just,
> > And makes me end, where I begunne.[2]

Critics concur this is "the most famous" metaphysical image,[3] noting it "is still today frequently cited as the perfect example of a 'metaphysical' conceit."[4] Others have stressed that it is not its mechanical nature, or even its oddity, that makes it metaphysical, but the way it achieves significance in the poem:[5] "Probably no other image is used so often to illustrate metaphysical poetry, and it might be well to point out that Donne has other interests than mathematics and navigation, and that his compasses do not necessarily involve a reference to some new science. What is more typical of metaphysical style is the way Donne extends and develops his initial idea, by arguing a series of parallels between the spiritually linked lovers and the joined legs of the compasses."[6] In light of these opinions, the study of a similar type of imagery in Spanish poetry adds a new dimension to that poetry and provides new points of departure for comparative studies.

The relative scarcity of mechanical imagery in Golden Age poetry results from a strong disdain for manual labor and a precept of propriety in the choice of poetical vocabulary. Spain has usually been regarded as hostile to

---

2   Herbert J. C. Grierson, ed., *Metaphysical Lyrics and Poems of the Seventeenth Century* (Oxford: Claredon Press, 1962), 15.

3   Helen Gardner, "The Metaphysical Poets," in William R. Keast, ed., *Seventeenth Century English Poetry* (New York: Oxford University, 1978), 38, and Earl Miner, "Wit: Definition and Dialectic," in Ibid., 52.

4   D. C. Allen, "Donne's Compass Figure," *MLN,* 17 (1956), pp. 256-7.

5   The first was James Smith, "On Metaphysical Poetry," in F. R. Leavis, ed., *A Selection from Scrutiny,* II (Cambridge, England: Cambridge University Press, 1968), 164.

6   James Winny, *A Preface to Donne* (New York: Charles Scribner's Sons, 1970), 139.

the seventeenth-century scientific revolution, a label that is never used by Spanish historians except to explain why such a movement failed to materialize there. Recent studies have shown that Spanish thought, while not on a par with the rest of Europe, was not as alien to the European scientific revolution as historians of science, still battling the Church's persecution of Galileo, liked to think.[7] The employment of technical imagery in Spanish poetry shows not only further interest in scientific advances, but in addition, a tendency towards a new more concrete way of conceiving of abstractions which can be taken as evidence of participation, if not in scientific speculation, at least in the same mode of thought that characterized it.

The study of science and technology developed in Spain in the sixteenth century on a par with the rest of Europe. The Spanish gained much practical technical knowledge in the development of their colonies, and they were leaders in the fields of ship-building, navigation and mine construction. The navigational treatises were especially popular in the rest of Europe, and the Casa de Contratación in Seville was instrumental in training seamen and developing methods of navigation. However, in the seventeenth century the various scientific academies disappeared and the empirical approach to scientific problems completely changed because of the revival of the scholastic method that stifled original investigation (López Piñero, 1979: 377-86).

The figure of Francisco Vallés (1524-1592), Philip II's personal physician, typifies this change (Ibid.,

---

[7] José María López Piñero, *La introducción de la ciencia moderna en España* (Barcelona: Ediciones Ariel, 1969), and José María López Piñero, *Ciencia y técnica en la sociedad española de los siglos XVI y XVII* (Barcelona: Editorial Labor, 1979).

344-5). As a humanist, he wrote commentaries on Hippocrates and Galen which relied heavily on linguistic interpretation of texts and explanation of the ancients. As a practitioner he exemplified the new experimental approach by relying on observation and practical experience to cure patients. As a theorist, he initiated the revival of neo-scholasticism. His treatise, *Controversia*, cited repeatedly by Spanish seventeenth-century doctors, was written in the form of the medieval *dubia*, a discussion of disputed theoretical propositions in which the author collects relevant opinions of authorities in order to "prove" one point or the other.

This book marked the beginning of a new era in Spanish science that would be characterized by long, dull, closely-reasoned treatments of impractical propositions. While the rest of Europe was beginning to observe, measure, weigh and experiment, Spanish philosophers returned to the medieval habit of citing authorities and disputing abstract metaphysical questions. This system of thought predominated in Spain in spite of some interest in scientific advances, especially in the eastern provinces, and it produced the backwardness that eighteenth-century thinkers, such as Feijóo, battled in order to integrate Spain into the main-stream of European thought.[8]

Part of the Spanish resistance to the scientific revolution in the seventeenth century can be seen in the attitude towards technology. According to the *Diccionario de autoridades*,[9] the very definitions of the words "mecánica" and "mecánico" expressed this low

---

8 Benito Jerónimo Feijóo, "Causas del atraso que se padece en España en órden a las ciencias naturales," in *Obras escogidas,* Biblioteca de autores españoles, vol. 56 (Madrid: RAE, 1952), pp. 540-5.

9 Real Academia Española, *Diccionario de Autoridades,* (Madrid, 1726-39; ed. facsl, Madrid: Gredos, 1963), 3 vols.

esteem. Any technical sense the words may have had is completely overshadowed by a disdain of manual labor: "Mechanica. Significa también la acción indecorosa y mezquina, propia de la gente baja y soéz: o la misma cosa ruin y despreciable. Lat. *Vilitas. Actio vilis, rudis, despicabilis.*" As an adjective, "mecánico" not only pertained to low class: "Se aplica regularmente a los oficios bajos de la república," but it also referred to the vile and gross: "Se toma también por cosa baja, soéz e indecorosa." Another noun, "Mechaniquez," had no technical sense, but expressed solely the loathing for the technical arts and those who practiced them: "La vileza o desdoro que resulta de ocuparse en cosas mecánicas." *Autoridades* gives another word, "machinaria" which had been coined by a seventeenth-century mathematician to express the good sense of technical achievement:

> Nombre que dan algunos modernos al arte llamado mechanica o Machinica, que es el que enseña la fábrica de tales máchinas, que pueda con ellas cualquiera fuerza levantar y mover cualquiera peso. El Padre Tosca tom. 3 pl 266. le da este nombre, para que le tenga diferente del que en nuestro vulgar idioma tienen las artes que no son liberales.

Juan de Pineda's etymology of "mecánica" casts a moral opprobrium over the useful arts:

> *Mecar* quiere decir adulterar..., y es palabra griega; y como el entendimiento haya sido criado para casar con las sciencias nobles, que llaman liberales por ser intelectuales, si dejadas éstas, se aplica a otras artes manuales, bajas y viles, indignas de él, dícese *mecar* o adulterar.[10]

Huarte de San Juan expresses the same loathing for manual work, claiming "ninguna cosa abaja tanto al

---

[10] Juan de Pineda, *Diálogos familiares de la agricultura cristiana,* III, Biblioteca de autores españoles, vol. 163 (Madrid: Ediciones Atlas, 1963), 276.

hombre como ganar de comer en oficio mecánico.''[11] He used his theories of the humoral or chemical composition of man to show that the Spaniards, because of their biological determinants, actually lacked the mental aptitude for the despicable and useless mechanical arts:

> ... los que habitan debajo el septentrión ... tienen mucha humidad y calor, por donde juntan gran memoria para las lenguas, y buena imaginativa, con la cual hacen relojes, suben el agua a Toledo, fingen maquinamentos y obras de mucho ingenio, las cuales no pueden fabricar los españoles por ser faltos de imaginativa. (206)

> ... la imaginativa de los que habitan debajo el septentrión ... sólo es buena para hacer relojes, pinturas, alfileres y otras bujerías impertinentes al servicio del hombre. (280)

These texts, along with many others that could be cited,[12] show a complete disdain for technical studies. This attitude, coupled with the revival of the scholastic method, signaled a turning away from scientific studies and the general course of European intellectual history.

The rejection of scientific imagery is also seen in painting. Unlike their northern contemporaries, Spanish painters tended to avoid images of scientific apparatus, suggesting that mechanical objects were not highly esteemed, nor their understanding a necessary acquirement of a gentleman. The disdain for mechanical arts was so great that painting itself was excluded from the liberal arts because the painter worked with his hands.[13] A few paintings do employ mechanical images, such as Valdés Leal's *In ictu occuli* and Pereda's *Sueño*

---

[11] Juan Huarte de San Juan, *Examen de ingenios para las ciencias,* ed. Rodrigo Sanz (Madrid: La Rafa, 1930), 320.

[12] Miguel Herrero García, *Ideas de los españoles del siglo XVII* (Madrid: Gredos, 1966), 96-7.

[13] Jonathan Brown, *Images and Ideas in Seventeenth-Century Spanish Painting* (Princeton: Princeton University Press, 1978), 106-9.

del caballero. Both paintings present a profusion of scientific apparatus, but they are included to make a moral point. They represent the vanities of the world that are to be despised precisely because they are subject to change and death. Instead of showing pride in learning and technical achievements, they preach a moral disregard for the mutable world of human affairs. Such symbolism actually disparaged the mechanical arts.

The disdain for mechanical arts resulted in an avoidance of language dealing with work. Dámaso Alonso demonstrated that many of Góngora's poetical figures, especially allusion and paraphrase, serve to avoid naming everyday objects.[14] E. M. Wilson has shown that the poetic commentators, from Herrera to Salcedo Coronel and Pellicer, censured words that smacked of the low class, and they faulted their heroes, Garcilaso and Góngora, for slips in decorum.[15] However, several poets, such as Quevedo, Soto de Rojas, and López de Zárate, purposefully chose the imagery of domestic tools, especially in religious poetry where the "shock" of the commonplace served to awaken the reader from a lethargic spiritual state and to recall that God was the author of everything, the exalted and the humble. The disdain for mechanical work and the rules of decorum provided nearly insurmountable obstacles to the employment of mechanical imagery. The fact that some poets did have recourse to this vocabulary to achieve concrete philosophical imagery shows its appeal in a generally hostile environment.

In spite of the attitudes disparaging mechanical arts

---

[14] Dámaso Alonso, *Estudios y ensayos gongorinos* (Madrid: Gredos, 1967), 92-116.

[15] E. M. Wilson, "La estética de Don García de Salcedo Coronel y la poesía española del siglo XVII," in *Entre las jarchas y Cernuda* (Barcelona: Editorial Ariel, 1977), 157-94.

and the rules of decorum, there existed powerful motivations for the utilization of mechanical imagery in poetry. One reason was that scientific theory in the Renaissance provided a series of fascinating analogies for expressing the veiled realities of existence. One such analogy was the theory of the correspondence of the microcosm and the macrocosm, which meant that the things of the physical world were designed to be visible signs of the larger unseen spiritual world. Thus, the elements and laws of nature were manifestations of higher spiritual realities.[16] Another analogy was based on the belief in a series of hidden sympathies and antipathies between the things of the world. Renaissance philosophers worked from the conviction that there existed "occult" forces of attraction and repulsion that could be harnessed and utilized by man.[17] These hidden forces created irresistible points of comparison for describing the force of love in human affairs.

Another reason for employing scientific imagery in poetry was that it could express relationships with greater precision. The technical advances of the scientific age provided a series of new instruments and a greater precision in the older ones on which the scientists depended: "... the one development that made possible the scientific revolution was the tremendous technological advance in the manufacture of precision instruments of observation and measurement, which furnished mankind with the telescope, the microscope, the micrometer, the barometer, the thermometer, the pendulum clock, and balances, no longer accurate to 1

---

[16] Francisco Rico, *El pequeño mundo del hombre* (Madrid: Editorial Castalia, 1970).

[17] Marie Boas, *The Scientific Renaissance, 1450-1630* (New York: Harper Torchbooks, 1962), 166-196.

grain but to 1/500 of a grain."[18] This imagery provided the illusion of precision for expressing abstract relationships.

The new technology was made more attractive by the limited nature of poetic imagery in sixteenth-century Spain, especially in the Italianate love poetry, which was conventionalized and often repetitive. Boscán and Garcilaso had introduced Italian metrical forms into Spanish, and with this revolution came the themes, images, and even the very phrases written in imitation of Petrarch and his followers in Italy. In spite of the excellence of Renaissance poetry, even that of minor poets, the corpus as a whole suggests repetition and stagnation. Herrera's verses are some of the most carefully sculpted in all Spanish poetry, and yet, taken as a whole, they give the impression of a ripe fruit on the point of decay. Gracián condemned the lack of variety in the Petrarchan poets: "Ni todo ha de ser jocoso, ni todo amoroso, que tantos sonetos a un asunto liviano, más sentidos que entendidos, en el mismo Petrarca, en el mismo Herrera, empalagan."[19] It is to the credit of Lope, Góngora, Quevedo, and the host of other poets of their period that they were able to take this rich inheritance and not only continue its excellence, but also instill into it a new and vital spirit. This renovation often appears to be more a continuation rather than the revolution that it actually was. The sense of continuity was achieved in large part through the use of the same metrical forms and by varying and intellectualizing the themes and images that already existed. On the surface, seventeenth-century poetry often looks and sounds like

---

[18] David Maland, *Europe in the Seventeenth Century* (New York: St. Martin's Press, 1967), 31.

[19] Baltasar Gracián, *Agudeza y arte de ingenio,* II, ed, Evaristo Correa Calderón, (Madrid: Clásicos Castalia, 1969), 255.

sixteenth-century poetry, but on analysis one sees the predominant poetical effects no longer issue from traditional rhetorical devices, but have been converted into wit and conceits. Gracián's very phrase "más sentidos que entendidos" provides the clue. Sixteenth-century comparisons often appeal to the senses alone, whereas seventeenth-century comparisons also function on an intellectual level, combining sensual appeal and philosphical thought. Also important were new themes and imagery, especially scientific imagery whose precision and intellectual nature gave it an attraction of its own.

The use of mechanical imagery in Spanish Golden Age poetry seems to be the outward and visible manifestation of an imperceptible and unconscious change of mental habit. A. C. Crombie maintained that the scientific revolution was preceded by a change in the mode of thinking and the type of questions asked: "In its initial stages, in fact, the Scientific Revolution came about rather by a systematic change in intellectual outlook, than in an increase in technical equipment."[20] He characterizes the change as "the geometrisation of space." The present study documents this change in intellectual outlook by showing that Spanish poetry reflects new mental habits and new ways of conceiving of ideas and relationships that resulted in a shift from rhetoric to concrete mechanistic imagery. This tendency is not extremely obvious in Spanish letters nor is it seen in all writers, but the fact that it is seen at all is significant in the evaluation of the Spanish Baroque.

The change is evident in the descriptions of a palace by Juan de Mena in his *Laberinto de Fortuna* and Villamediana in his *Fábula de Faetón*. Juan de Mena's

---

[20] A. C. Crombie, *Medieval and Early Modern Science,* II (New York: Doubleday Anchor, 1959), 122.

narrator is abandoned in a desert where he sees the palace of Fortune. The title of the stanza suggests a technical description: "Enarra el número de la casa de la Fortuna," but in fact the description is more rhetorical:

> E toda la otra vezina planura
> estaba cercada de nítido muro,
> así trasparente, clarífico, puro,
> que mármol de Paro paresce en alvura,
> tanto que el viso de la criatura,
> por la diafána claror de los cantos,
> pudiera traher objectos atantos
> cuantos celaba so sí la clausura.[21]

Mena captures the effect of the building by describing its brightness and accumulating references to light: "nítido, trasparente, clarífico, alvura, claror, and diafána."

Unlike Mena's description which emphasizes the light and the effect of the building on the viewer, but leaves the actual shape, size and style to the reader's imagination, Villamediana dwells on the geometrical forms of the palace:

> El gran palacio del señor de Delo,
> sobre asiento lustroso colocado,
> en recto ángulo cuadro está en el cielo,
> de líneas espirales coronado;
> feliz labor en inmortal desvelo,
> émulo fue del jónico cuidado;
> del superior metal arde la puerta
> a la meta de Alcides descubierta.
>
> Los ámbitos que informan el tablero
> —distinta proporción en paso grave—,
> del sitio circulando el grueso entero,
> hace que el eje en sus convexos trabe.

[21] Juan de Mena, *Laberinto de Fortuna,* ed. John G. Cummins, (Madrid: Ediciones Cátedra, 1979), 62.

Paralelos describen el crucero
en simétrica planta, cuya nave
en serie igual contiene, desiguales,
brillantes frontispicios arcuales.[22]

Like Mena, he refers to the light: "lustroso" and
"brillantes," and he also mentions many other elements,
such as the workmanship: "feliz labor en inmortal
desvelo", the materials: "superior metal," the style:
"jónico," and the ornamentation: "frontispicios
arcuales." The main thrust of the the two stanzas,
however, is to place the building geometrically and
establish its shape. The description continues over some
sixty stanzas, but these two give the first impression of
the palace, dwelling on its geometrical aspects. It is
seated "en recto ángulo cuadro" and topped with "líneas
espirales," and has other geometrical qualities:
"proporción," "circulando," "eje," "convexos,"
"paralelos," and "simétrica planta." These words
place a great deal of emphasis on the geometrical shape
and placement of the building, an element that was
completely lacking in Mena's description.

Even though fifteenth-century poets are known for
the abstract nature of their poems, their intellectualizing
is more rhetorical and hence different from that of the
seventeenth-century poet whose abstractions tend to be
based on concrete imagery, if not geometrical and
scientific notions. The fact that the seventeenth-century
poets preferred this type of imagery parallels a similar
change in philosophical and scientific outlook, and for
that reason it achieves importance in the history of ideas.
That Sor Juana Inés de la Cruz used the pyramid as the
central image of her *Primero Sueño* can hardly be called

---

22   Juan de Tassis Peralta, Conde de Villamediana, *Obras,* ed. J. M.
Rozas, (Madrid: Clásicos Castalia, 1969), 215.

scientific, but on the other hand, that seventeenth-century writers and thinkers were looking for, and found, geometrical archetypes and mathematical explanations for physical and mystical phenomena shows a common intellectual perspective that in one of its many manifestations resulted in the modern scientific movement.

Science played a much reduced role in the life of the seventeenth-century Spaniard than it did in the rest of Europe. Regarding applied science and technology as part of the dishonorable mechanical arts, most Spaniards strove to show their gentlemanly breeding, and therefore despised tools, industry and technical knowledge. The study of science reached an all-time low in the seventeenth century in Spain when the progress based on empirical studies in the sixteenth century was lost in the revival of the scholastic method that produced a stagnation in Spanish scientific advances until the introduction of foreign ideas in the last part of the seventeenth century, a movement that culminated in the writings of Feijóo and the eventual absorption of foreign science in Spain. The outstanding advances of the sixteenth century in navigational science and in mining came to a halt in the seventeenth century as the scholastic philosophers fell into the worst excesses of belabored metaphysical speculation. In spite of these changes, some Spanish poets continued the tradition of the appreciation of scientific advances, and produced a small corpus of poetry that corresponds in many respects to the metaphysical poetry of northern Europe.

2. Baroque Imagery

The role of the image in Baroque art is highly significant. The word "baroque" itself often suggests a profuse visual image of scrolls, cherubs and cartouches. Beyond being an age that preferred visual imagery in its art and daily life, it was also a period when imagery in certain circles assumed a deeper and, at times, mystical significance. Kepler conducted his very exact astronomical observations for the purpose of finding archetypal imagery in the universe. Also popular were types of imagery based on mystery, such as the didactic emblem and the poetic conceit. In many cases, this imagery provided a means of linking very disparate elements and imbuing new life into traditional concepts. Before studying the role of mechanical imagery in Spanish Golden Age poetry, it is necessary to examine the concept "Baroque" and the function of imagery in Baroque poetry.

Characteristic of Spanish Baroque art is an abundance of ornamentation, an almost fanatical desire to fill every space with exuberant imagery and tense movement. Likewise, the poetry shows a marked tendency towards an accretion of rhetorical devices and imagery. The calm balance of Renaissance art gave way in the Baroque to a contorted montage of ingenious poetic devices. The abundance of devices is noteworthy not for their novelty but the special way in which they are employed. In his studies on Góngora, Dámaso Alonso observed that there are very few rhetorical effects that do not also occur in Garcilaso, Fray Luis de León, Herrera,

15

and other sixteenth-century poets.[1] The difference is the number and manner in which Góngora employs them. Even very common devices, such as metaphor, metonymy and hyperbole, are accumulated in a way that strikingly parallels the profusion of classical motifs in Baroque architecture. Gracián must have been one of the earliest writers to note the similarity between Baroque architectural imagery and the rhetorical devices in poetry: "Cada piedra de las preciosas, tomada de por sí, pudiera oponerse a estrella, pero muchas juntas en un joyel, parece que pueden emular el firmamento; composición artificiosa del ingenio, en que se erige máquina sublime, no de columnas ni arquitrabes, sino de asuntos y de conceptos" (I, 63).

The term "Baroque" is commonly used to designate two quite different artistic phenomena. Most often it refers to a highly ornamented style of architecture, but also includes late seventeenth- and early eighteenth-century musical ornamentation, the paintings of Rubens, and the ornate poetry of Marino and Góngora. For very different reasons, Velázquez is called a Baroque painter. In his case, "Baroque" indicates, rather than a love of ornamentation, a play of perspective and a complexity of form. By analogy, one sees similar structural complexity in the buildings by Bernini and the church of San Sebastián in Madrid, as well as in metaphysical and *conceptista* poetry. To cover the dichotomy of this terminology, it seems best to adapt to a Spanish context the definitions given by Warnke in his study *Concepts of Baroque* (1-20). He defines Baroque as a period in which there flourished two major styles: the High Baroque and the Metaphysical. In

---

[1] Dámaso Alonso, *Góngora y el "Polifemo"* (Madrid: Editorial Gredos, 1967), I, 165.

Spanish literature, the harmony and balance of the Renaissance style are transformed around the beginning of the seventeenth century into the various Baroque styles, all of which have as main characteristics a sense of imbalance and conscious distortion of harmony and proportion, be it far-fetched comparisons, abstruse references, contorted syntax, or hyperbole. While both styles have these elements in common, the High Baroque utilizes them for the effects of pomp and sumptuous decorative motifs, whereas the Metaphysical style in a more realistic vein extracts from them a conceptual and paradoxical message. It is the difference between Góngora's *Soledades* and Quevedo's *sonetos morales,* the difference between the *culterano* and *conceptista,* if we realize that these two terms describe tendencies and are not mutually exclusive categories.[2]

By and large it is the metaphysical and *conceptista* style in the Baroque that utilizes mechanical imagery and uses the images to extract conceptual paradoxes about man's existence. No study of imagery in the seventeenth century can divorce itself from the phenomena of *conceptismo.* As Gracián makes clear, *conceptismo* is an intellectual art written not for the senses, but for the mind: "De suerte que se puede definir el concepto: Es un acto del entendimiento, que exprime la correspondencia que se halla entre los objectos" (I, 49). The introduction of *conceptismo* into Spanish seventeenth-century poetry produced several breaks with the Renaissance traditions in the employment of imagery. In the first place, it prescribes that the image not be simply sensual or visual, but, since it is a part of conceptual art, it must be intellectual in nature. Thus, even though the image may

---

[2] Andrée Collard, *Nueva Poesía. Conceptismo, culteranismo en la crítica española* (Madrid: Editorial Castalia, 1967).

17

be visual, it will also have an intellectual level, not only savored by the senses, but understood by the mind.

Seventeenth-century *conceptismo* relies on a far-fetched comparison of two terms that have little to do with each other and are related only through an ingenious connection. The seventeenth-century conceit is appreciated, not for its abstruse language, but for the ingenuity and wit of the comparison. The Jesuit poet and teacher, Casimir Sarbiewski, used the triangle as a structural model for the conceit. The base of the triangle (line AB) is the material from which the poet takes his witty ideas. One line leading to the tip of the triangle represents similarity (concordia) and the other is dissimilarity (discordia), and the tip (C) is the conceit or point of correspondence that allows for a comparison juxtaposing the dissimilar and the similar in a figure that seems more striking than just.[3]

Even though the words *image* and *imagery* have clearly defined semantic fields, their meaning in critical terminology is not at all clear.[4] In modern usage, they are usually defined as any concrete representation of a sense impression. In traditional rhetoric, and for some modern critics, an image consists of a comparison in which both elements compared are mentioned: "sus dientes eran menudas perlas" (D. Alonso, 1967, I, 165). In modern English terminology, this is a metaphor employing concrete imagery, but in traditional rhetoric, it is not a metaphor because in a metaphor proper only the second element of the comparison is present: "...que entre perlas y corales respira,"[5] where the reader must supply teeth

---

[3] Casismir Sarbiewski, *Praecepta Poetica* (Krakow, 1958), 12.

[4] P. N. Furbank, *Reflections on the Word 'Image'* (London: Secker and Warburg, 1970).

[5] Fernando de Herrera, *Obra poética,* I, ed. J. M. Blecua (Madrid: RAE, 1975), 347.

and lips from his knowledge of poetic conventions. Lapesa presents this dichotomy clearly, for he defines an image as "toda representación sensible," but in the subsequent explanation, he qualifies the definition, recalling the older idea of a comparison: "...presta forma sensible a ideas abstractas o relaciona, combinándolos, elementos formales de diversos seres, objetos o fenómenos perceptibles."[6] In many handbooks of literature, the definition of image vacillates between signifying any sense impression and a figure, like metaphor, that relates diverse elements.

The dichotomy present in these definitions actually reflects a change in the use of poetic imagery. As Rosamund Tuve conclusively demonstrated,[7] the function of imagery in sixteenth- and seventeenth-century poetry is not to evoke feelings and reproduce the poet's personal experience as it often is in Romantic and Modern poetry, rather it signifies and defines in a precise manner, reinforcing the stated theme and meaning of the work. The older rhetorical definition of image as a comparison corresponds more clearly to its use in poetry before the Romantic period, and its more modern definition as a representation of an object perceived by the senses describes its looser function in modern poetry.

The vagaries in the definition of "image" and the limited bibliography on the subject do not create insurmountable obstacles for constructing a model for the study of the structure of mechanical imagery. The restriction of this study to the Baroque period and to a specific type of imagery imposes sufficient limitations to

---

6 Rafael Lapesa, *Introducción a los estudios literarios* (Madrid: Ediciones Cátedra, 1974), 45.

7 Rosamund Tuve, *Elizabethan and Metaphysical Imagery* (Chicago: University of Chicago, 1968).

arrive at a structural model. Since the image in sixteenth- and seventeenth-century poetry has a denotative function, that is, it is compared to another term, idea, image, etc., it consists of two parts: (1) the sense representation or image proper, which I call the sign, and (2) a another term or concept to which it is compared, which I call the figure.

This leaves unsolved the problem of how an image comes to have significance. The art historian E. H. Gombrich has defined the problem of imagery clearly and succinctly: "Images apparently occupy a curious position somewhere between the statements of language, which are intended to convey a meaning, and the things of nature, to which we only can give a meaning."[8] Baroque imagery and emblems lie in this indeterminate region between having fixed meaning and no meaning whatsoever. In the case of mechanical imagery, the poet often arbitrarily assigns a meaning to an incidental feature of the image based on a casual correspondence. Other times, the image itself has a symbolic meaning which the artist reinforces with new relationships. For these reasons there exists a tension in the image between the types of correspondence linking the sign to the figure.

Even though the most interesting part of the structure of an image, and the one that holds the most promise for the study of metaphor and conceit in general, is the understanding of the correspondence, modern critics have ignored this area of research. Twentieth-century critics have used two criteria for evaluating and classifying the conceit: (1) the legitimacy of the comparison drawn and (2) its function in the poem. Both of these criteria stem from Dr. Johnson's criticism of the metaphysical poets in his "Life of Cowley." The first

---

8   E. H. Gombrich, *Symbolic Images* (Oxford: Phaidon, 1978), 2.

idea was formulated by Johnson as a criticism of the conceit and the second evolved as a defense of the conceit against this criticism. Johnson said the metaphysical poets used far-fetched and extravagant comparisons, and he criticized them for departing from nature and the true order of things. Undoubtedly he would have granted that all comparisons involve a falsification. Hair is not strands of gold, but since one can easily transfer the appropriate qualities of gold to blonde hair, the comparison neither shocks nor seems unnatural. Dr. Johnson was referring to the type of comparison that falsifies the nature of one or both of the terms involved. He gave as an example Cleveland's comparison of the sun to a coal pit (Johnson, 1967: 29). Using this criteria, Dr. Johnson argued that comparisons are of two types, those that correspond to the natural world and those that falsify nature.

The second classification of the conceit probably arose as a defense of certain writers against the accusation of unnatural comparisons. Modern critics have distinguished between the decorative conceit and the organic or functional conceit.[9] The former is a comparison that works only on a superficial level and has no deeper conceptual meaning. The organic or functional conceit serves to justify the use of a false comparison because it does establish a deeper meaning.

None of these considerations were the concerns of seventeenth-century rhetoricians or theoreticians. Traditional rhetoricians established the categories of rhetorical figures based on the type of relationship between the tenor and vehicle, such as synesthesia, substitution of one sense impression for that of another; synecdoche, naming the part for the whole or vice versa,

---

[9]   K. K. Ruthven, *The Conceit* (London: Methuen & Co., 1969), 5-7.

or metonymy, naming one part for another. Following this lead, Gracián's study of *agudeza* classifies conceits and intellectual imagery by the type of correspondence found between the two terms of the figure. Since the conceit is based on a conceptual or intellectual comparison, he classified the types according to the categories of logic, such as analogy, contradiction, etc.[10]

Gracián also presents another aspect of wit that is important for the study of imagery, what he calls "líneas de ponderación." By this, he means that there are multiple correspondences between certain terms; however, in the case of Baroque imagery, it seems to be more systematic than Gracián allowed for. In fact, every image seems to be composed of at least two lines of correspondence, one usually on a sense level and the other on an intellectual level. His inclusion of *semejanzas,* contraries, and other types of sense comparisons in his classification seems to confuse the two levels. Few conceits rely solely on the logical connection so clearly perceived by Gracián. An example of a purely intellectual and logical correspondence is found in a sonnet by Quevedo: "Azadas son la hora y el momento."[11] This comparison is startling not only because of the introduction of a commonplace tool "azada" which more elegant writers would have censured, but also for the extravagance of the comparison. Unlike roses in the cheeks or pearl-like teeth, the metaphor "spades = hour and moment" needs elucidation. The correspondence is found on an intellectual level with no sense connection whatsoever. It

---

10 A. A. Parker, in Luis de Góngora, *Polyphemus and Galatea* (Austin: University of Texas Press, 1977), outlines the various types of logic correspondences.

11 Francisco de Quevedo, *Obras completas,* ed. J. M. Blecua (Barcelona: Editorial Planeta, 1971), vol. I, 5.

is a correspondence based on analogy, that is, the spades serve the same function as the divisions of time in that each one prepares our funeral monument. While this comparison is purely conceptual, most conceits show more than one correspondence, often of different types, between the two terms, such as in Lope de Vega's comparison of a shepherd's staff to the cross: "tú que hiciste cayado de ese leño / en que tiendes los brazos poderosos."[12] The text mentions the point of sense correspondence (the two objects are made of wood) that makes the rest of the comparison possible. Taken by itself the sense comparison is somewhat ridiculous; the real meaning behind the comparison is conceptual. It is an "agudeza por proporción" or analogy because each object is functionally an instrument of salvation, so that the real correspondence is Christ's love of man and His desire to save him.

Mechanical imagery in poetry and emblematic imagery are similar because both use an image as a point of departure for establishing the meaning. In addition, the emblem is an excellent analogy because its parts are of different genres. It consists of a pictoral image, which properly is enigmatic, and a poem which provides clues for the meaning of the emblem. Theorists of the emblem called the image the body and the poem the soul, thus, the two, image and poem, body and soul, form and elucidate the complete emblem.[13] In like manner, the seventeenth-century poetic image consists of two distinct parts, the image proper, or the sign, and the comparison, or figure.

[12] Lope de Vega, *Rimas sacras,* in *Obras poéticas,* ed. J. M. Blecua (Barcelona: Editorial Planeta, 1969), vol. I, 323.

[13] Aquilino Sánchez Pérez, *La literatura emblemática española* (Madrid: Colección "Temas," 1977), 20.

In actuality, however, each image, and each emblem, is composed of three parts, the two terms called the sign and figure, and the veiled correspondence between them. Sarbiewski's triangles serve as a clear model for the seventeenth-century image. In the triangle, there are two paths from points A and B: the single line AB and the double line ACB. In most images, there are two types of correspondences: a simple link, based on some sense impression, which, because it is based on a non-essential or secondary characteristic of the object, I call the accidental correlation, and a conceptual correspondence, which is the intellectual aspect of the comparison and its real *raison d'etre*. Occasionally there may be more than two lines of correspondence, but even so, they fit into these two categories. Even though in Lope's sonnet the shepherd's staff and the Cross do not resemble each other, the comparison involves multiple lines of correspondence. The accidental correlation, based on the fact that both are made of wood, provides a point of superficial relation, and the conceptual correspondence concerns their function: Christ, the Divine Shepherd, uses the Staff to direct his flock to salvation just as Christ's sacrifice on the Cross is the salvation of mankind. Thus the comparison, even though not plausible on first reading, is in fact justified on two different levels.

The accidental correlation can be classified into four categories: (1) similitude, (2) equivoque, (3) archetype, and (4) antithesis. The similitude is a sense comparison like that of the Cross and the staff, based on some visual, audible, or material correlation between them. Quevedo concludes one of his famous sonnets on the brevity of life with the phrase "pañales y mortaja juntos" (4). The accidental correlation, based on the similitude that both are made of cloth, allows for the juncture, but the main

24

intention lies not in the sense impression, but rather in the analogical function. The two cloths serve to cover the new-born and the dead, thus they bring the extremes of life, birth and death, together, joining them in one terrible moment.

Another fine example of similitude comes from an anonymous passage cited in Gracián:

> Hipócrita Mongibelo,
> nieve ostentas, fuego escondes.
> ¿Qué harán los humanos pechos,
> pues saben fingir los montes? (I, 107)

The image compares the sign, a volcano, to the figure, the lady's breasts, without referring to the obvious similitude that both have conical similar shapes. The poem establishes several other lines of visual correlation. The mountain is hypocritical because it has snow on its surface, but hides volcanic fires inside. In the same way, the lady keeps an icy appearance, but hides, like the mountain, her fiery passion inside. Another accidental correlation based on similitude may be posited from the fact that the complexion of the lady's breasts are snow white. From these visual similarities, one understands why the mountain and lady are hypocritical, and the conceptual correspondence consists of realizing, that like the mountain, the lady's cool exterior is feigned. In this case, part of the delight arises from the fact that the most obvious correlation, the shape of the mountain and the breasts, is rather risible, and contrary to the reader's expectation, the poet leaves it unstated in order to develop other details that lead to the conceptual correspondence.

The equivoque is a play on words in which the poet establishes the accidental correlation by using a word in two different senses. This then allows for the conceptual correspondence on the intellectual level. A passage from Quevedo, cited in Gracián, in which Apollo addresses the fleeing Daphne shows this structure:

> Ya todo mi bien perdí,
> ya se acabaron mis bienes,
> pues hoy, corriendo tras ti,
> aun mi corazón, que tienes,
> alas te da contra mí. (I, 70)

"Alas del corazón" refers to the valves of the heart and metaphorically indicates courage and spirit. Apollo argues that since Daphne has his heart, she uses "alas," that is, both wings and spirit to flee from him. On the level of the accidental correlation, the "agudeza" is allowed because "alas" refers to the heart he has metaphorically given to her and to wings as an aid in flight. On the level of the conceptual correspondence, his pursuit and love only served to spur her on. Gracián had reservations about this figure. He said Quevedo speaks "con más sutileza que cultura." The lack of "cultura" undoubtedly indicates the use of familiar language and the indecorous reference to a technical part of the body, not the word play itself.

An example that is based on two equivoques occurs in a poem by Rodrigo Artes y Muñoz in which he shows in the image of the clock the elements of good government: "cuerda, aunque no tirante, es su justicia."[14] This involves a double word play. First, "cuerda" is used equivocally as a noun to refer to the chord or chain used to wind the clock and as an adjective to modify the governor's sense of justice as sane. The one word sets up

---

[14] Joseph Delitalá y Castelví, *Cima del monte Parnaso español con las tres musas castellanas Caliope, Urania y Euterpe* (Caller: Onofrio Martin, 1672), 123.

the accidental correlation, "chord equals justice" and allows for the deeper sense "justice is sane." In the second equivoque, he uses "tirante" to modify the chord (it is not a pull chord) and to modify justice (it is not tyrannical). "Cuerda" and "tirante" both are used equivocally to refer to clock parts and to justice. The accidental correlation is a word play, but the deeper correspondence, which is definitely not explicit in the image, sees good government as a well-regulated clock.

The third category of accidental correlation, the archetype, includes several types of association, all based on an already established relation, be they written texts, proverbs, or clichés. It includes the examples in Gracián's chapter "De los conceptos por acomodación de verso antiguo, de algún texto o autoridad" (II, 62-8). This "new wine in old skins" reestablishes a previous idea or text, but infuses it with new material. The accidental correlation is the fact it has been stated before, and may even be well known, but the conceptual correspondence provides a new link between the two terms.

Francisco de la Torre y Sevil wrote a series of sonnets on an hourglass whose sands were the ashes of a deceased beautiful lady. The first sonnet revives the old association "vivir = morir." Originally this correlation was one of the fourth type based on antithesis, but the two terms had been juxtaposed so many times that they had been reduced to a dull cliché. Torre y Sevil revived that cliché by infusing it with a new conceptual correspondence: "para enseñar que así muere la vida, / así con inquietud vive la muerte."[15] On the conceptual level, the hourglass by showing the passage of time

---

[15] Juan Oven, *Agudezas,* trans. Francisco de la Torre [y Sevil] (Madrid: Francisco Sanz, 1674), 391.

teaches how life is a slow death. Because the ashes are in constant movement, the lady restlessly lives out her death. This very literal sense infuses new life and freshness into a well-worn association.

Torre y Sevil creates a similar comparison in the second sonnet on the same subject. He claims that the "reloj de arena," because of the ashes of the lady, is in fact a "reloj de sol":

> Reloj eres del sol, cuando corriente
> índice de ceniza es el que asombra;
> de sol, porque de Nísida, aunque ausente. (392)

The accidental correlation is seen in the third line where he explains that the sign, "reloj de arena," becomes a figure, "reloj de sol," because the hourglass is composed of the deceased lady. This correlation is based on a well-worn comparison of the mistress to the sun. Originally, of course, it was a correlation of similitude: the mistress is shining, beautiful, radiant, etc., but none of that is evoked here because the poet simply recalls the cliché, which serves to justify the conversion of the hourglass into a sundial. The absence of the lady in death heightens the correlation by proclaiming the absence of the sign. The conceptual correspondence occurs in the first two lines which explain that both have the same function: the sands are a flowing pointer that surprise us with the passage of time. The concept is, of course, less exciting than the correlation, but that is typical of the minor *conceptistas* who give greater emphasis to the more superficial accidental correlation than to the profounder implications of the conceptual correspondence.

This type of correlation is a favorite one in the Baroque because it allows for the reiteration of tradition, and at the same time, since the conceptual correspondence is original, it infuses new life into the traditional. This is important in the treatment of mechanical and geometrical imagery because it permits the poet to reaffirm on new terms the older ideas that may no longer be valid as descriptions of the physical world. These comparisons can result in a synthesis of the out-moded and the latest innovation. Lope de Vega finds in geometrical imagery the image of the divinity of man:

> Si al triángulo santo que contiene
> tu círculo divino, el pensamiento,
> tal vez como veloz, confuso viene,
> en mi pequeño mundo mira atento
> tu semejanza, pues el alma tiene
> memoria, voluntad y entendimiento. [16]

The use of geometrical imagery is something of an innovation in seventeenth-century poetry, although as Manuel Morales Borrero has shown,[17] the image of the circle is common in Golden Age religious poetry. Lope draws an image of a circle within a triangle. The circle is the symbol of perfection, and hence represents the perfection of the divinity. There are several archetypal correlations in this image: man as an image of the macrocosm, the perfection of the circle, the number three representing divinity, and the image of the Trinity in man's psychological faculties. The correspondence is less obvious. The saint believes that because of his disordered thoughts his Lord may not be able to

---

[16] Lope de Vega, *El cardenal de Belén,* in *Obras,* ed. M. Menéndez Pelayo, Biblioteca de Autores Españoles, 177 (Madrid: Ediciones Atlas, 1964), 177-8, also used in Lope de Vega, *Los Pastores de Belén,* in *Obras escogidas,* vol. II, ed. Sainz de Robles (Madrid: Aguilar, 1973), 1505b.

[17] Manuel Morales Borrero, *La geometría mística del alma en la literatura española del Siglo de Oro* (Madrid: Fundación Universitaria Española, 1975).

recognize the creature made in His image. He recalls a number of archetypal images in order to convince the Divinity of his holy intention. Thus, the correlations are employed to reaffirm the individual's position in the order of the universe.

I have called the last category of accidental correlation antithesis. It covers two different types of correlation. The first is an actual antithesis based on opposition between the sign and figure. The second is not a real antithesis, but arises from an intentionally unsettling lack of similarity in the comparison. The first type is seen in two conceits by Góngora in praise of a collection of holy relics: "mudo coro / de muertos vivos."[18] The first image consists of an adjective and noun whose individual sense is precisely opposite. Although one can conceive of a choir not singing, the word "mudo" often signifies something permanently silent. The correlation of the image lies in the intentional juxtaposition of two concepts that are in fact opposites. The second image "muertos vivos" is even more clearly of the same type, for the combination of the two is a logical contradiction. The correspondence in both cases explains the juxtaposition. The relics displayed on the shelves are now a part of the Heavenly choir, but being relics, they are mute. The relics are "muertos," but in this case, since they have been canonized, they definitely are alive in the Heavenly sphere. While the correspondences consist of a juxtaposition of elements from different categories, the correlations are based on the fact that the terms are contraries.

I have included in the category of antithesis not only images that use terms that are exact opposites, but also

[18] Luis de Góngora, *Sonetos completos*, ed. Biruté Ciplijauskaité (Madrid: Clásicos Castalia, 1969), 70.

those that set up an opposition between the terms because of a absence of any logical connection between them. In the example explained previously in which Quevedo compares spades to the hour and moment is a case in which the terms are not opposites, but are in fact antithetical because they lack a logical connection. Of the same type is the image from the last line of a sonnet by Lope de Vega to San Diego: "pues hacéis entender que el pan es rosas" (Gracián, I, 106). The opposition and discord between the sign and figure definitely produce a surprise for the reader. The very lack of a logical connection leads to the question: how can bread be roses? The correspondence in this case involves a play on words. The bread is a special type, the Eucharist, and roses is a colloquial expression meaning everything is fine. The very lack of a logical connection serves as the reason for joining the two terms, making the reader pause and search for a logical association.

The model also serves to explain clearly the difference between a functional and a decorative construction. A functional image has both the accidental correlation (even if it is nonexistent because of antithesis) and the conceptual correspondence, but a decorative image lacks the deeper conceptual level. On the surface, both sound alike because they are often strained far-fetched comparisons, but the decorative image lacks any deeper meaning. Torre y Sevil's poems on the ashes of the dead mistress in an hourglass provide a clear example:

> Tú eres la que ya desvanecida,
> cada hora en su túmulo aun la aclama,
> y en las ciegas memorias de mi llama
> más que en tus claros senos repetida. (392)

He says the hourglass proclaims hourly the death of the lady in her tomb and in his blind memories more than in the transparent breasts of the hourglass. The comparison of the bulbs of the hourglass to the breasts of the lady is purely decorative. The concept of his feeling the passing hour more in his memory than she in the hourglass is already established. The "claros senos" are simply a periphrastic expression for the glass of the container. The correlation is superficial with no deeper sense. The example of similitude discussed earlier which compared breasts to a mountain peak did provide an intellectual depth for the understanding. The image of Torre y Sevil consists of an extravagant comparison, but the reader learns nothing new either about hourglasses or about breasts. Since it lacks a conceptual correspondence, its function in the poem is purely decorative.

The uniqueness of Baroque imagery rests on several qualities. In the first place, it imparts an intellectual comparison, and secondly, it usually consists of two levels of comparison, one on the level of sense impressions and the other on the level of intellectual comprehension. And finally there is an interplay between the two levels of correspondence. The creation of the structural model clarifies several points about Baroque imagery, and may eventually be capable of elucidating the diverse functions of Baroque metaphor. Dividing the parts of correspondence into two or more levels and defining the types of accidental correlations makes clearer how the image is both comparison and dissimilarity at the same time.

3. Metaphysical Poetry in Spain

In present critical terminology, metaphysical poetry refers to a group of English seventeenth-century poets and a number of continental writers of the same period whose work is characterized by intellectual imagery, colloquial expression, and rough rhythms.[1] At the beginning of the twentieth century it was used as a term of praise for all intellectual poetry and the best modern poets. With the revival of Donne and his contemporaries, the term was restricted to a number of seventeenth-century English poets, but later extended to include continental poets of the same period. Among these, Quevedo is most often singled out because his style resembles that of Donne, the prototype of metaphysical poetry.[2] Except for Quevedo, this style had a limited diffusion in Spain. Warnke's anthology of metaphysical poetry includes poems by Quevedo and Sor Juana Inés de la Cruz, and religious sonnets by Lope de Vega. He comments on the two peninsular writers:

> ... the Metaphysical combination of conceit, colloquialism, and paradox, markedly present in the devotional poetry of Lope de Vega and Quevedo, seems largely absent from Spanish love poetry. The one important exception to this

---

[1] See Warnke, 1974. The *Encyclopedia of Poetry and Poetics,* eds. Alex Preminger, F. J. Warnke, and O. B. Hardison, Jr. (Princeton: Princeton University Press, 1965), 495, defines it as "distinguished by ingenuity, intellectuality, and, sometimes, obscurity."

[2] See Kelley and L. Elaine Hooker, *John Donne and Francisco de Quevedo. Poets of Love and Death* (Chapel Hill: University of North Carolina Press, 1978).

33

> generalization is Francisco de Quevedo, many of whose amorous lyrics combine concrete particularity and intellectual complexity in a manner fully characteristic of the Metaphysical style. ... Apart from the work of Quevedo himself, the movement produced little Metaphysical poetry on secular themes. (Warnke, 1974: 52-3)

The hostile attitude of seventeenth-century Spaniards towards science and technology seems to account in part for the comparatively small output of metaphysical poetry. The rejection of mechanical and scientific notions as debasing and ignoble and the precepts mandating the decorum of the traditional high style served as obstacles to the use of commonplace words and the creation of the concrete imagery necessary to the metaphysical style. In spite of its limited extension, it is possible to see an interest in the metaphysical style in several writers, such as Quevedo, López de Zárate, Lope de Vega, Soto de Rojas and Bocángel, at the beginning of the seventeenth century.

Many of the poems treated in this study can be classified as metaphysical either because of their use of concrete imagery or because of the thematic material they extract from the imagery. The poems are of varied quality. Some are admittedly trivial and superficial, others of a type of *conceptismo* considered abhorrent while others are well-known masterpieces. Since the majority of the poems can be classified as metaphysical poetry, this study serves to document the diffusion of this style in Spain.

One important aspect of metaphysical poetry is the emphasis on originality. Renaissance rhetoricians had inherited Aristotle's definition of poetry as imitation, and this definition, coupled with the Latin concept of imitating established masters, produced a theory of poetics that verged on sophisticated plagiarism and denied originality to the artist. Several theoreticians were quite uncomfortable with the concept of imitation, but the majority conformed to the traditional definition. Gracián's *Agudeza y arte de ingenio* is proof of a de facto change of direction, for if the poet is prided on the subtlety of his concepts and comparisons, these must be original and not copied from other writers, or if they are traditional comparisons, they must be compared on new grounds. Even though most sixteenth-century poets show originality, the Italianate poetry of the Renaissance forms a very unified and at times restricted whole. There is a uniformity of vision and expression in its topics and imagery that must have been problematical for seventeenth-century writers. There is indeed a difference in poetical practice between the two centuries, and even though Gracián does not reject imitation outright, it is obvious that *conceptismo* signifies a new poetic theory based on originality.

Another important aspect of metaphysical style is the use of a great diversity of correspondences in the poetry. This occurs with such regularity that it must be an intentional effect. It is one of the first beauties of the conceit that Gracián extols. In the first chapter he laments the lack of variety in earlier poetry, and the type of variety he specifies is diversity of correspondences: "Cénsuranse en los más ingeniosos escritores las agudezas, antes por unas, que por únicas, y homogéneos sus conceptos: o todos crisi, o todos reparos, correlaciones o equívocos; y es que falta el arte, por más que exceda el ingenio, y con ella la variedad, gran madre de la belleza" (I, 49). This is an important aspect of Baroque poetry, for the numerous types of correspondence are startling, and the effect occurs with such frequency that it cannot be accidental.

The intention of the metaphysical poem to surprise

and rouse the reader by unusual effects makes the variety of poetic recourses difficult to classify. Startling effects can be achieved in a number of ways, such as the use of colloquial expressions, disrupted syntax, extravagant comparisons, and unresolved paradoxes. The poems employing mechanical imagery are of two general types. Some are constructed around the parts of one central image which is given a sharp conceptual twist at the end, making the reader reflect back and reinterpret the imagery and comparisons. Others develop an argument through difficult and abstract comparisons that are distinctly unrelated to each other. The second type is probably more common, but is less prevalent in this study because many of the poems discussed here are developed around a central mechanical image. Since the metaphysical aspects of Quevedo's poetry have been treated elsewhere (Kelley, 36-152), I have chosen examples by other poets.

Typical of the type of poem employing an extended image is a sonnet by Pedro Soto de Rojas, most of whose poetry cannot be considered metaphysical at all. Some of his earlier poems, however, present images of the humbler sort that suggest the metaphysical mode. In one sonnet, when his mistress retires to a village, he imagines himself a laborer of love: "Aunque en vez de escarpín, y guante estrecho / bejigas calce el pie, llagas la mano" (67).[3] Paradoxically, love which should ennoble has come to degrade the lover and corrupt his sense of decorum. He now must pull love's ponderous triumphant chariot: "Desde hoy (Bootes de esa luz) me emplea / amor al carro perezoso junto, / y sin

---

[3] Pedro Soto de Rojas, *Obras,* ed. Antonio Gallego Morell (Madrid: CSIC, 1950). In all quoted poems, I have modernized the spelling, added accent marks, and occasionally modified the punctuation. In the following sonnet I have added the "a" in line 6 to facilitate the reading.

dispensación mi dulce asunto, / azada, reja, y hoz, quiere que sea" (66-7). The humble imagery, commonplace vocabulary, playful paradox, and rough syntax are typical of the metaphysical style. Elsewhere he employs imagery from the forge, a burning house, and similar concrete objects.

Soto de Rojas' most sustained metaphysical poem is the sonnet "Reo, y Fénix disculpada" (published in 1623, but with a "privilegio" de 1614). The central image presents the poet as a sculptor, using a chisel to transpose his thought into marble. Although this image became something of a cliché in the romantic period, it is a great deal fresher in the seventeenth century when tools and work with the hands were despised. Soto de Rojas also used the chisel in another remarkable image expressing the futility of his love: "que intento / labrar en bronce con buriel de viento" (73). The sonnet "Reo, y Fénix disculpada" has the same vigor of expression, and the imagery is not at all trite as it builds conceptually to the last line, which reveals the full force of the paradox:

REO, Y FENIX DISCULPADA

No alcanza el buen cincel un pensamiento
que no posible a solo un mármol sea,
si docta mano en imitar se emplea
conceto agudo, a sano entendimiento.

Ya rendida si opuesta al movimiento,
la materia, [a] la forma que la afea,
delito es vil de torpe mano rea,
culpado ingenio, cómplice instrumento.

Labrar quise en tu pecho mi ventura,
dispuesto a buena estaba y mala suerte:
erré (como ignorante) la escultura.

No te quiero culpar, ¡o mármol fuerte!
Quiero culpar mi ingenio, y mi locura,
pues sólo supe en ti formar mi muerte. (46)

The octave produces a complex sign of a sculptor failing to realize his ideas in stone. In the first quatrain, the poet argues that it is indeed possible for a sculptor to achieve the expression of his thought in stone, if he has a trained hand, a clear idea, and is of healthy mind. In spite of the possibility, the poet tells us in the second quatrain that in this instance he failed to beautify the stone, which resisted the chisel and was disfigured by his idea. Instead of a "docta mano," the poet used a "torpe mano rea," and his "ingenio" did not create the witty conceit he desired. Even though it is possible to create a fine sculpture, the poet's mind, hand, and tool combined to produce a base work, and actually committed a crime.

The sextet provides two different figures for the sign of the marble from which the poet tries to carve a statue. In the first figure, the stone in whose heart the poet wished to carve his destiny is a sign for his beloved, who bears the name "Fénix." The accidental correlation of this image is based on an archetypal comparison of the beloved to stone because of her coldness and hardness. Since this correlation is a cliché, the poet artfully leaves it unstated. The thrust of the argument occurs on the conceptual level which infuses it with a new literal sense: the creation of love is like a work of art which can beautify crude unformed stone, creating an eternal monument. Developing further implications of this correspondence, the poet-lover does not blame the marble, the lady, but rather his own intentions. Instead of employing a "docta mano" he erred as an "ignorante." His "locura," the folly of his intention, contrasts with the "sano entendimiento" (line 4) necessary for a successful outcome.

The first figure for the stone statue is his mistress, and at the end of the poem, he introduces a new figure, his own death. Throughout, the poem carefully builds to the new figure, the last word, "muerte." Instead of a beautiful statue, the poet has only been able to create his own death. The second figure for the central image comes as a surprise causing the reader to reflect back and reinterpret its elements. The accidental correlation for the figure "muerte," like the previous correlation, is also a cliché, used conventionally to indicate a lover's suffering, but here of course the stone is cold and dead—no other result could have been expected. Not only does the image provide a literal correlation for the old cliché, it also works on a conceptual level which picks up and ties together several threads of argument, and at the same time gives them a new dimension. It works on several levels. First is the concept of "reo" from the title. As a criminal he has only been able to fashion his own death sentence. The lady, who had nothing to do with his love, will get off scot-free, but the poet, who wished to carve a destiny in her heart, has been found guilty and condemned to death (suffering). The second correspondence recalls the lifelessness of the stone. He has been able to carve only an inanimate image—create a scornful mistress. For this reason, the whole idea was wrong from the start, and he blames his foolhardiness in trying to create life from cold unwilling stone. Typical of metaphysical poetry, the poet brings out the paradoxes and falseness of the conventions of traditional poetry.

This poem is unusual in that it consists of only one extended image which is used twice to give it greater depth. The poet has taken several commonplaces of courtly love poetry, the lady's heart is as cold and hard as stone and the lover's trials are like death, and he has infused new life into them through concrete imagery that turns on itself and points out the futility and deception of out-worn conventions. The precision of the imagery and its ability to express a complex set of psychological ideas make this a fine metaphysical poem.

Lope de Vega's sonnet 51 of his *Rimas sacras* is a good example of a religious poem in the metaphysical style constructed around a central image:

> Descalzo el pie sobre la arena ardiente,
> ceñida la cabeza de espadañas,
> con una caña entre las verdes cañas,
> que al Tajo adornan la famosa frente,
>
> tiende sobre el cristal de su corriente
> su cuerda el pescador, y por hazañas
> tiene el sufrir que el sol por las montañas
> se derribe a las aguas de occidente.
>
> Sale a su cebo el pez en tal distancia,
> mas, ¡oh gran pescador, Cristo, ceñido
> de espinas, que, en la caña de tu afrenta,
>
> sacas del mar del mundo mi ignorancia,
> el pie en la cruz, ribera de mi olvido,
> para que el cebo de tu sangre sienta![4]

The poem develops colorful realistic details the archetype of the Evangelical metaphor of the fisher of men's souls: "And he saith to them: Come ye after me, and I will make you to be fishers of men" (Matthew 4:19).[5] The idea of Christ as bait with which to entrap the devil was developed by the Church fathers, and became something of a commonplace.[6]

Rather than announce the allegory at the beginning, Lope uses the octave to present the sign of the fisherman in very realistic terms. He evokes the local setting of the Tagus, the details of the fishing pole and line, and the glare of the setting sun off the water late in the day. The

---

[4]   Lope de Vega, *Rimas sacras,* in *Obras poéticas,* 341-2.

[5]   All Biblical quotations come from the Douay version: *The Holy Bible* (London: The Catholic Truth Society, 1963).

[6]   Meyer Schapiro, "'Muscipula Diaboli,' The Symbolism of the Mérode Altarpiece," in Creighton Gilbert, ed., *Renaissance Art* (New York: Harper Torchbooks, 1970), 23.

exactness of the imagery and the humbleness of the details, such as the fisherman's bare feet, are surprising in the context of Spanish Baroque poetry.

All the details in the octave are signs that are linked to their figures in the sextet. In the central image, the fisherman is a sign for Christ. The accidental correlation for this one extended image is an archetypal idea based on an Evangelical text. The correspondences are worked out in the many details of the allegory of the poem, several of which are purely decorative, functioning only on the level of the accidental correlation and not having a conceptual correspondence of their own. Even though they are not functional on their own account, they serve to amplify the main image of Christ the fisherman.

The bare foot on the sandy banks of the Tagus becomes Christ's foot on the cross. The comparison is made possible by the placement of the bare foot on each. Conceptually, the shore, like that of the river of oblivion, and the cross represent the role the sinner's neglect plays in the Lord's death. But the foot on the cross, like Christ standing on the bank fishing for souls, serves to awaken the sinner from his moral stupor. The strange detail of the "espadañas" which crown the fisherman's brow are a sign for the crown of thorns, an image based on an equivoque: the sharpness implicit in the name "espadaña" serving to link it to the "espinas" of the crown. The fishing pole, picked from the rushes of the river bank, is subject to two possible interpretations. If it is one of the reeds of the flagellation, then the image is simply decorative, adding details to the central image. The second possibility is more interesting. If it is the cross, then the accidental correlation is remotely plausible since both are instruments and both are made of wood. The fact that they do not resemble each other in the slightest in form or shape is overcome by the conceptual correspondence which is based on function, and which Gracián would have called an "agudeza de proporción." The pole will pull the sinner from the sea of humanity and sin, just as the cross delivered man from original sin.

The red reflection of the sunset, which strikes his eyes, suggests Christ's death through suffering, but in fact the image is very complex. The red glare cast on the water by the setting sun has three distinct correlations to Christ's crucifixion. The redness foreshadows the blood; the painful glare from the water is the suffering of martyrdom; and the setting of the sun is an "hazaña" symbolizing the death of the Lord. The sextet produces the conceptual correspondence. The redness becomes the blood of Christ, the very bait that awakens the sinner from his dangerous indifference. The image of Christ's blood as bait for the salvation of man had been previously developed by Saint Augustine in one of his sermons,[7] but is cleverly incorporated by Lope into the full context of the image of the fisherman. The Lord Himself is the bait on the pole-cross that attracts man to salvation.

In addition to the exploitation of a single image with multiple meanings, the sonnet displays two other characteristic elements of metaphysical religious poetry. First, the concreteness of the imagery, and secondly, the conceit based on a paradox. Man's salvation is presented as a seizure rather than an escape from the pleasures of the world in which the Saviour offers himself as the bait to save man. This comparison, an "agudeza por contrariedad," as Gracián would have classified it, compares fish who are caught and killed to man who is caught and made to live. Probably because of the long

---

[7]   Ibid., and Cornelius a Lapide, *Commentarii in Mattheo*, 4:19.

traditions of Biblical exegesis, the metaphysical style in religious poetry is characterized by more extravagance of image and metaphor, a greater disparity between the sign and figure, and at times, multiple and varied lines of correspondences between them. This poem clearly contains all of these elements. Lope incorporates previous Biblical exegesis into the wit of his poem. Not only are several comparisons far-fetched (the fishing pole as cross), but several are exploited for multiple purposes (the sunset as blood, suffering, and death). Even though based on a single image developed in all its realistic humbleness, the sonnet uses the parts of the image as springboards to other transcendental ideas. While typifying a poem based on a single image, it also shows other aspects of metaphysical religious poetry.

The other general category of metaphysical poetry is based on a central argument in which several unrelated images and metaphors are adduced to establish the validity of the main thesis. A fine example of this type of poem is the following sonnet by Góngora (dated August 23, 1623):

DE LA BREVEDAD ENGAÑOSA DE LA VIDA

> Menos solicitó veloz saeta
> destinada señal, que mordió aguda...
> agonal carro por la arena muda
> no coronó con más silencio meta...
>   que presurosa corre, que secreta,
> a su fin nuestra edad. A quien lo duda
> (fiera que sea de razón desnuda)
> cada sol repetido es un cometa.
>   Confiésalo Cartago, ¿y tú lo ignoras?
> Peligro corres, Licio, si porfías
> en seguir sombras y abrazar engaños.
>   Mal te perdonarán a ti las horas,
> las horas que limando están los días,
> los días que royendo están los años. (239)

Góngora's name is so closely associated with the "culterano" style that it seems odd to consider him as a writer of conceptist metaphysical verse. However, like Lope de Vega, he successfully experimented with a number of styles, such as the *romance* and the *letrilla*. This sonnet, besides being one his finest creations, represents an experiment in the metaphysical style of Quevedo. Even though the sonnet demonstrates several characteristics of Góngora's "culterano" style, such as violent hyperbata, neologisms and Classical allusions, these effects are used to intellectual ends and the final result resembles more the dense style and rough rhythms of the metaphysical poets than it does the poetry of Góngora and his followers.

Like a metaphysical poem, this sonnet is discursive and argumentative, rather than descriptive, and its imagery and comparisons are cerebral rather than sensual. It achieves its effects through the use of direct address, colloquial expressions, disrupted syntax, and extravagant concrete comparisons. The images are characterized by their intellectual nature, their varied and tangential relationship to the central idea, the development of incidental or casual meanings, and a hidden correspondence between the sign and the figure. For these reasons it stands out in Góngora's production as atypical. Salcedo Coronel in his commentaries on Góngora's sonnets singled it out for two reasons: its use of commonplace examples and its didactic nature: "Trata de la brevedad de la vida, comprobando con ejemplos la verdad que experimentamos cada día, y persuadiéndose con ellos a despreciar los engaños y vanidad de este mundo. Es uno de los más sentenciosos y elegantes sonetos que escribió don Luis" (509-10).[8]

---

[8] García de Salcedo Coronel, *Obras de Don Luis de Góngora comentadas*, II (Madrid: Diego Díaz de la Carrera, 1644), 509-10.

Gongoristic poetry is usually narrative or descriptive, and its metaphorical and conceited language points ultimately to an underlying meaning.[9] In contrast, this sonnet presents a straightforward argument in which the concrete images carrying the burden of the argument give the impression of being randomly selected and form a disparate surface, but combine on another level to form a succinct argument.

The octave presents three basic metaphors, all of which represent the deceitful brevity of life. Many editions seem to break the unity of these metaphors by reading lines 5 and 6 as a new and separate sentence. Modern editions of Gracián's *Agudeza y arte de ingenio* clearly separate them off by using exclamation marks and accents on the words "que."[10] I believe, however, that the two phrases in lines 5 and 6 beginning with "que" actually finish the comparisons begun in line 1 with "menos" and in line 4 with "más." For that reason, I have used suspension points after "aguda" and "meta" to indicate the interruption of the phrases which are only resumed in line 5. The first image thus completed is the quick arrow seeks its target with less speed than our pressured age and life run to their end, and the second, the chariot does not round the goal post more silently than our quiet age runs to its end. "Presurosa" and "secreta" modify "edad," but also refer back conceptually to the "veloz saeta" and "silencio," that is to say, the first image presents the end of life as coming

[9] John R. Beverley, *Aspects of Góngora's "Soledades"* (Amsterdam: John Benjamins B. V., 1980); R. O. Jones, "Neoplatonism and the *Soledades*," *BHS*, 40 (1963), 1-16; and R. O. Jones, "Góngora and Neoplatonism Again," *BHS*, 43 (1966), 117-20.

[10] Baltasar Gracián, *Obras completas*, ed. Arturo de Hoyo (Madrid: Aguilar, 1967), 293, and *Agudeza y Arte de ingenio*, ed. Evaristo Correa Calderón (Madrid: Editorial Castalia, 1969), I, 144.

swiftly and the second image emphasizes the silence and surreptitiousness of the end. This reading contradicts Salcedo Coronel's interpretations of the second image, since he saw both images as referring to speed: "Valióse don Luis de esta segunda comparación para ponderar la velocidad con que corre nuestra edad al último termino de la vida" (511). The second image, however, has no reference to speed, but the words "muda" and "silencio," reinforced by "secreta" in line 5, overwhelmingly identify it as an image of silence.

The three basic images of the octave are not at all related to each other, but serve to make intellectual points: (1) death comes more quickly than an arrow seeks its target and (2) more silently that a chariot in the Roman arena would make the perilous turn around the goal post before a hushed audience. Every intelligent person recognizes this because (3) every passing sun is a perilous foreboding of fleeting time and death. The three basic comparisons are not at all connected to each other, but each one is isolated and introduced to illustrate a part of the argument, and even though the figures are based on correlations through similitudes their essential relationship to their signs is conceptual. The arrow, even though the poet alludes to its biting sharpness, is present to conceptualize velocity. The games present the idea of silence, and the sun-comet serves less as a visual image than a portentous symbol of disaster. These images argue forcefully for (1) the brevity of life, (2) the silence with which death approaches, and (3) the inevitable and visible passing of time which signifies man's personal demise.

The function of the imagery cannot be reduced to such a simple set of values, for Góngora exploits all possble relationships and meanings from it. He extracts from the images other complementary meanings that

46

seem to be almost accidental but are carefully woven into the Baroque texture of the poem. These secondary meanings serve to reinforce on different levels the idea of the brevity of life, particularly the deceptive, but all-pervasive presence of death. The arrow that violently strikes its target is probably intended for us. "Agonal" is a neologism that refers to a Roman festival, but in Spanish it sounds like and suggests "agonizar," to be dying. The "arena muda" strikes us as strange. The traditional interpretation of these lines is that "muda" actually refers to the anticipatory silence of the unnamed audience. Strictly speaking, it is a transferred epithet in which "muda" is applied to sand, but is really meant to modify the hushed audience. In this case, the transference of the epithet is not merely decorative, but serves to underline the basic argument of the sonnet. The silent sand recalls the sands of the hourglass which quietly slip through the neck of the timepiece and mark the passage of time. In addition, Salcedo Coronel interpreted the "meta" as "el extremo de la vida..., o la misma muerte" (511). Thus on another level, the "agónico carro" is converted into a magnificent chariot, representing the triumph of death in the very moment it approaches the goal of life, death itself, its movement recorded in the silent sands of time which mark its irrevocable course.

The complexity of the syntax is used to reinforce the idea of death. The adjectives, "presurosa," "callada," and "aguda," do not read easily in their sentences. They seem to serve the function of adverbs, but the adverbial ending *-mente* is missing, and they do not end in *-o* as would the short form of the adverb. Their form is clearly adjectival, but in their position and sense they seem to modify verbs. One wants to read in the text "mordió agudamente" and "corre presurosa y secretamente,"

47

even though "aguda" must modify "saeta" and the last two modify "edad." Along with the misattributed adjective "muda," all of these feminine adjectives are syntactically dislocated to the point that their very function is dubious. I would suggest Góngora has placed, or misplaced, these words in order to suggest that one feminine noun that is missing from these lines, and which one suspects will enter and tie them all together: the figure of death, La Muerte, the feminine noun, always unnamed, that lurks behind these verses just as it haunts man's existence. Typical of the metaphysical poet, Góngora plays on many incidental aspects of language and imagery. The disrupted syntax, the striking lack of parallel constructions, and the multitude of relationships between the signs and figures all serve to reinforce the central argument. The exploitation of these seemingly random devices for intellectual ends is typical of the metaphysical poem, especially one that employs a number of images.

The third image in the octave completes the impending sense of doom. It seems to be a visual image: each passing sun is like a comet. The visual and astral correspondence is quite obvious, but it is in reality a comparison that the poet means for us to understand on an intellectual level. In Gracián's terminology, it is an "agudeza por proporción," that is, an image based on analogy. Each passing of the sun marks our time, and thus serves as a reminder of our impending and final doom, just as the appearance of a comet foreshadows a great disaster. Thus, the real comparison is of an intellectual nature based on the function of the comet which presages disasters. The poet observes that the sun also has the same function in that it presages our own destruction. Even though the visual similarity gives the comparison a justness that is pleasing, it is incidental to the real basis of the comparison.

The thought is dense and the syntax contorted in the octave, but the sextet is straightforward and plain-spoken. Cartago recalls the theme of ruins, and needs no further development. The name Licio in Góngora's moral poetry refers to the poet himself. The "sombras y engaños" characterize this world and its hollow pleasures. In the last two images, the destructive nature of time is characterized by the abrasive hours that wear away the days and the rodent days that gnaw away at our existence, converting the shadows and falsehood of this world into the ruins of once great cities. The accidental correlations of these two images are based on antithesis: hours do not resemble files nor days gnawing rodents. The conceptual correspondences, time as a destroyer, carries the weight of the image. Our "edad," (line 6) be it our own personal existence or the man-made things of the world, is silently, but surely, decaying. These last two images were highly praised by Salcedo Coronel (515) and were probably the "agudezas por semejanza" which Gracián praised in his *Agudeza y arte de ingenio* (I, 144).[11] Both writers express a great excitement about these comparisons; Salcedo Coronel states he imitated them in one of his verse epistles.

In spite of Góngora's reputation as a High Baroque poet, this sonnet is an excellent example of a poem in the metaphysical style that uses a variety of images and poetic devices to present a central argument. Lack of consistency and balance is apparent throughout, but probably the most disparity is seen between the rough syntax and dense contorted expression of the octave and the clear flowing, even lyrical, tone of the sextet. Both parts of the poem use conceits, but the images and

---

[11] Gracián seldom indicates the conceit he wishes to point out, but simply quotes the whole poem.

metaphors of the first part are so constructed as to generate second and third levels of meaning that in turn reinforce the central argument of the poem. It remains a brilliant *tour de force* in which Góngora ably competed with Quevedo's dense "conceptista" style. Not only does it serve as an excellent example of a certain type of metaphysical poem, but it is indeed a masterwork of Spanish literature.

The poems analyzed in this section, along with others that might be included, are evidence of a wider diffusion of the metaphysical mode at the beginning of the seventeenth century in Spain than previously allowed, especially among minor poets. It is not necessary for the purposes of this study to delve into the sources of this poetry or to explain how a style could seemingly cross language barriers and exist in several countries at the same time. The examples in this chapter show how the various types of metaphysical poems work and how the poet weaves into the concrete imagery the philosophical paradoxes of man's earthly existence. Many of the poems studied in this monograph will not only show the importance of scientific and mechanical thought in Spain, but they will also serve as evidence of further diffusion of the metaphysical style.

PART II

Technical Instruments

4. The Balance Scale

The balance scale provides a good point of departure for the study of mechanical imagery in seventeenth-century poetry. Since the simple instrument is heavily charged with traditional symbolic meanings of justice, it illustrates the use of imagery that relies on a traditional meaning and at the same time takes a new direction by introducing more mechanical properties of the device. Some poets utilize the traditional symbolical meanings, but actually make their point based on the mechanical properties of the scale, while others abandon all sense of symbolism and employ the scale solely as a mechanical illustration of their ideas.

The balance scale is a very old device, with evidence of its existence dating from ancient Sumerian and Babylonian cultures. The very first references to the balance show that the metaphor of weighing one's deeds as a means of determining the value of life seems to be nearly as old as the instrument itself. An illustration in the *Book of the Dead* (c1200-945 B.C) shows the god Anubis weighing a heart on a carefully constructed scale.[1] *The Book of Job* (ca. sixth or fifth century B.C.)

---

[1]   George Sarton, *A History of Science,* I (Cambridge, Massachusetts: Harvard University Press, 1952), 54, 80.

speaks of weighing one's moral character to determine his worth: "Let him weigh me in a just balance, and let God know my simplicity" (31: 6). The image was particularly popular in Medieval art because the scale was associated with the Last Judgment. The third seal in Revelations reveals a mounted horse: "And he that sat on him had a pair of scales in his hand" (6: 5). This was always interpreted as the apparatus for determining those worthy of salvation and those deserving condemnation.[2] Medieval frescos often depicted St. Michael the Archangel weighing the souls of the dead, and, since the Last Judgment often graced the tympanum of the church doors, the balance scale can be seen in sculpture also, as above the doors at the Cathedral of León.

The concept of divine judgment continued into seventeenth-century art, and is seen in Valdés Leal's *Finis Gloriae Mundi,* which represents the corruption of the earthly after death. The bottom of the painting depicts a gloomy crypt with opened caskets displaying three bodies in various stages of decomposition. In the middle of the dark crypt, above the decaying bodies is a balance scale suspended by a hand coming from the top of the painting. Each pan holds seven animals: the ones on the left symbolize the seven deadly sins, and the letters below read "ni más," and the animals on the right symbolize the seven cardinal virtues and the letters read "ni menos." The location of the judgment above the corrupting bodies points to the spiritual permanence of the afterlife and the importance of morality. Even though one might question the propriety of such a painting for the chapel of a hospital, the significance of the balance scale is obvious and clearly traditional; it is

    2 Cornelius a Lapide, *Commentaria in Scriptorum Sacrum,* XXI (Paris: Ludovicus Vives, 1891).

weighing the works of man's life in the final judgment of his days on earth.

The balance scale is not only a symbol of divine judgment, it is also a symbol of earthly justice, the scale representing the fairness and balance with which the courts reach a decision. The modern personification of justice as blindfolded and carrying a balance comes from the iconography of the goddess of justice, Astrea, the daughter of Truth, who ruled over the mythical golden age and fled to Heaven at its end. Her attributes are a balance scale, representing equality and fairness, and a sword, representing punishment. Covarrubias in his *Emblemas morales* presents the figure of justice with her sword and scales in Book III, Emblem 15. He makes no mention of the scales in the explanation; they are only symbolic attributes of the personification of justice.[3] Góngora and Jáuregui, among others, refer several times to Astrea and her scales, never in a technical sense, but only as a symbol of justice. Góngora uses them in praise of a patron of the "toga": "A quien por tan legal, por tan entero / sus balanzas Astrea le ha fiado" (81). Juan de Jáuregui shows the diffusion of this symbolism by referring to the attributes of justice without mentioning the goddess: "Este, por ejercer a maravilla / justicia y equidad, severo y blando, / hoy rige su balanza y su cuchilla."[4] These references are purely symbolic and in no way rely on mechanical notions.

The balance scale is such an ancient tool and so charged with symbolism that it may seem out of place in a study of seventeenth-century technical imagery. In spite of its commonplace use as a symbol throughout

---

[3] Sebastián de Covarrubias Orozco, *Emblemas morales* (Madrid: 1610; fcsml rpt, Menston, Yorkshire: The Scholar Press, 1973), Bk III, Emb 15.

[4] Juan de Jáuregui, *Obras,* ed. Inmaculada Ferrer de Alba (Madrid: Clásicos Castellanos, 1973), I, 53.

history, it assumes in the seventeenth century a nature quite different from that of the past. It comes to be used to portray intellectual and spatial relationships more characteristic of the metaphysical mode and baroque subtlety than of purely symbolic uses of the image. The word "balanza" had several meanings in Spanish which enriched its possibilities as a poetic word. According to the *Diccionario de Autoridades,* it could refer to the pans used for weighing, as in the expression "dos balanzas," or it could refer to the whole scale itself, including the pans. Metaphorically it could signify equilibrium, and in "germanía" it referred to the gallows. The last meaning probably came not only from the visual resemblance of the cross bar and upright, but also from the fact the scale could tip rapidly to one side, raising one pan upward, just as the gallows leave the victim suspended. Also, "fiel," signifying the equilibrium of the scale, was the source of further word plays.

In a sonnet criticizing the justice system, Quevedo employs the balance as a traditional symbol, but his use of the imagery shows a new tendency, since he evokes several mechanical properties of the balance to make his point. As a satirical commentary on the lack of equanimity of justice in his time, he slyly suggests that the goddess Astrea discard her balance, the symbol of fairness, since there is no equality in justice. She need keep only her other attribute, the sword, because it is the only one she uses.

PERSUADE A LA JUSTICIA QUE ARROJE EL PESO, PUES USA SOLO DE LA ESPADA

Arroja las balanzas, sacra Astrea,
pues que tienen tu mano embarazada;
y si se mueven, tiemblan de tu espada:
que el peso y la igualdad no las menea.
No estás justificada, sino fea;
y, en vez de estar igual, estás armada;

54

feroz te ve la gente, no ajustada:
¿quieres que el tribunal batalla sea?
Ya militan las leyes y el derecho,
y te sirven de textos las heridas
que escribe nuestra sangre en nuestro pecho.
La parca eres, fatal, para las vidas:
pues lo que hilaron otras has deshecho
y has vuelto las balanzas homicidas. (48-9)

The sonnet is based on the single image of the balance as a symbolic attribute of justice, but to show the inappropriateness of the symbolism, Quevedo recalls the mechanical movements of the scale. He says the scale is not moved by weight and justice, but shivers with fear of the harsh vengeance of the sword. Line 5 plays on two senses of the word "justificada," meaning justified and also possessing interior grace for salvation. Since the goddess lacks a sense of justice, the poet assumes she lacks God-given grace and labels her ugly. In the first tercet he skillfully plays on the meanings of "derecho" as law and righteousness. Thus, laws (leyes) are pitted against law (derecho) and righteousness, and the legal precedents are written in the blood of the victims. Astrea, instead of serving justice, is one of the fates, cutting off the thread of law spun out over the ages, and of course the image of death is implicit as she cuts the thread of life. In the last line the poet returns to the image of the balance, giving it a new figure, as he accuses the goddess of turning the scales into instruments of death. The accidental correlation is established through two equivoques, one on the word "balanzas," in the slang meaning of gallows, and the second on the verb "volver" in the sense of to become. On the accidental level, he says that because of the goddess the balance has become (vuelto) a tool of death (gallows), but on the conceptual level, the words have a different meaning and we understand she has tipped (vuelto) the scale to the side of punishment.

Quevedo does not speak of guilt or innocence or of weighing one's crimes to achieve justice. He criticizes the justice system in his time for being too harsh, for always tipping the scales against the accused. The balance scale is employed chiefly in its symbolic value of weighing one's crimes against his merits; however, this symbolism is negative, since he emphasizes the totally inappropriate character of the symbol, and suggests they are more an instrument of death than of equality. Even though the use of the symbol is proclaimed as non-traditional from the start, the image of the balance is employed in a symbolic fashion rather than as a tool for measuring the relationships between two objects. The humorous word plays, the concrete imagery, the short accusatory phrases punctuating the rhythm, and the repeated effect of the abrupt caesuras on "-al" in "igual" (line 6), "tribunal" (line 8), and "fatal" (line 12) establishes a counter rhythm typical of the metaphysical mode. Even though the image of the balance adds an air of concreteness, it does not yet show the fine observation of mechanical detail characteristic of other poetic uses of the image.

Like Quevedo, the emblematist Francisco de Villava places the balance ambiguously between its traditional symbolic meanings and an image with which to make concrete an abstract idea. His emblem shows a balance supported by a hand protruding from a cloud.[5] The pans of the balance hold a sword and a feather, and the scale is inclined towards the side of the feather. The commentary explains the double interest in the emblem. He says that the goods of the world were taken back to Heaven after Adam's sin, and following the prevalent

---

[5] Francisco de Villaba, *Empresas espirituales y morales,* (Baeza: Fernando Díaz de Montoya, 1613), 19r.

theories of syncretism in his epoch, he says this is represented in pagan myth by the legend of Astrea:

> Por ventura por esto fingieron los antiguos fabulistas que la virgen Astrea le volvió al cielo, por quien significaban la justicia, la cual, según su razón universal, significa y abraza todo género de bien. (19v)

Astrea is introduced because of an archetypal correlation between the balance scale and justice. Justice is one of the supernatural gifts returned to man through Christ's sacrifice, a comparison based on two archetypal texts, the Bible and the Christian interpretation of pagan myth:

> Y esto es también por ventura lo que apuntó Virgilio, aunque en otra ocasión, por lo que había oído de los versos de la Sibila Cumea, que en su tiempo volvía ya la virgen Astrea, y los dorados reinos de Saturno, que fue un justísimo rey. (20r)

However, the conceptual correspondence comes from the mechanical properties of the balance, that is, as one pan is lowered, the other rises by an equal degree:

> No hallé con que significar este pensamiento, sino en dos balanzas, que al inclinarse la una, se levanta y retira la otra, con que demás de significarse que cuanto bajó Dios subió el hombre, se representa vivamente que estando los bienes celestiales a cargo de su misericordia y los males de pena ni mas ni menos al de su justicia pesaron tanto en el tribunal del cielo los de su misericordia (por la que tuvo del hombre) que al inclinarse y bajar el soberano hijo, los males de su justicia se fueron retirando y huyendo como en efecto pasó. (20v)

The image of the balance expresses with precision the relationship between Christ and man—the humiliation of God for the exaltation of man. To the purely mechanical image, Villava has added archetypal correlations based on the traditional symbolic values of the instrument. Undoubtedly, the synthesis of traditional symbol, pagan myth, and ingenious metaphor based on observation was pleasing to the Neo-Platonic humanist looking for unifying correspondences between the world and Heaven.

The following images which present the balance in its function of weighing move further away from the traditional symbolism. The author of *La Estrella de Sevilla* uses the balance as a device for visualizing abstract concepts through the concrete imagery of the balance:

> Su honra en una balanza
> pone; en otro poner puedes
> tus favores y mercedes,
> tu lisonja y tu privanza;
> y verás, gran señor, cómo
> la que agora está tan baja
> viene a pesar una paja,
> y ella mil marcos de plomo.[6]

Don Arias explains to the king that Busto Tavera may seem very grave and serious because of his honor, but he cynically suggests they corrupt the young man with royal favors. His seriousness will, when weighed against the prestige of power and favor, prove to be unsubstantial. The success of the image depends on the fact that honor is an abstraction, and even though it gives one a grave and heavy demeanor, in the final result, it is weightless, and hence can come to weigh less than the more appealing flattery of the king's gifts. Even though the king is employing the scales, they are no longer, as the play demonstrates, a symbol of justice, but a tool of corruption.

Miguel de Barrios (Daniel Levi Barrios, 1635-1701) also uses the image in a sonnet praising "Los tres mártires de Sevilla," three conversos who were victims of

---

6 Anonymous, *La estrella de Sevilla,* in H. Alpern and J. Martel, *Diez comedias* (New York: Harper and Row, 1939), lines 457-464.

an Inquisitorial *auto de fe.* The sextet adapts imagery from *Isaiah* 40:12 praising the greatness of the Lord: "Who hath measured the waters in the hollow of his hand, and meted out heaven with the span. And comprehended the dust of the earth in a measure, and weighed the mountains in a scale, and the hills in a balance."[7] The meaning of the image is evident in the Biblical quote, but the word for *measure* has caused problems. It is translated into English from Hebrew as a measure, without reference to the type of measure, or the essential three of the Hebrew word. The *Vulgate,* the Casiodoro de la Reina translation, and the Douay all refer to measuring the dust with three fingers. Barrios, in the title of the sonnet, cites the passage, translating it as a triangle: "con triángulo cogió el polvo de la tierra." The ambiguity of what type of measure the number three refers to in this passage provides the basis for the word play and subsequent imagery of the sextet:

A LOS TRES MARTIRES DE SEVILLA

> Isías 40: "con triángulo cogió
> el polvo de la tierra," etc.

> Su polvo de Jacob Sevilla encierra
> y ve Isías que el Señor del cielo
> con los tres mide el polvo de la tierra.
> Inclínales el fiel de empíreo vuelo
> en la balanza de la ardiente guerra
> por pesar su ceniza más que el suelo.[8]

The delicate fabric of this poetry can only be appreciated by noting the subtle word plays and the Biblical

---

[7] *The Holy Scriptures According to the Masoretic Text,* II (Philadelphia: The Jewish Publication Society of America, 1955), 1040-41. I would like to thank Professor Alan Avery-Peck of Tulane University for helping me with the Hebrew in this passage.

[8] Kenneth R. Scholberg, *La poesía religiosa de Miguel de Barrios* (Madrid: Ohio State Univ., n.d.), 241-2.

references woven into the overall texture. As in the case of an archetypal correlation, the Biblical texts have been infused with new meanings. "Su polvo de Jacob" comes from a Biblical phrase extolling the greatness of the Hebrew people: "Who can count the dust of Jacob?" (Numbers 23:10). But in the context of Barrios' poem the dust of Jacob has become the ashes of the "martyrs," and the inability to count them refers not to the greatness of the creator, but to the greatness of the three victims. The poem continues with a second translation of the passage from Isaiah quoted as an epigraph. In the title, it is a triangle, but in the poem it approaches the Vulgate rendition of three fingers. Barrios lets the essential three of the Biblical quote become a substantive so it can refer to the three martyrs whose ashes, when weighed against the dust of the earth, prove to be heavier. Because of the specific context of the poem, the quote takes on a new meaning in which the poet glorifies the martyrs of the faith in place of their maker.

The second tercet continues with an oblique reference to the passage in Isaiah by developing the image of the balance scale from the conclusion of that passage. Like the previous tercet it is based on the conceit that the worth of these three warriors lends a weight to their ashes. "Fiel" seems not to mean balance here, but counterweight, and probably is intended to bring to mind the steadfast faith of the martyrs. "Empíreo" is a favorite word of the Baroque for the Heavens. "Ardiente" refers both to the ardor of the struggle of the martyrs and to their death by fire. "Ceniza" is usually a figurative expression for death and decay, but here it takes on the very literal sense of the remains of the burnt martyrs. This is a very rich and ingenious poetic text weaving into its fabric two paraphrased Biblical quotations and a number of word plays based on the imagery of the quotation. The balance is an essential part of the Biblical passage, but the poet has completely transformed it to his own purposes, a clear example of an archetypal correlation with a new meaning.

Sor Juana Inés de la Cruz uses the balance as an extended image in a sonnet on hope and despair. She presents optimism as a chronic illness that makes her life drag on, instead of falling into despair and ending it:

SOSPECHA CRUELDAD DISIMULADA, EL ALIVIO
QUE LA ESPERANZA DA

Diuturna enfermedad de la Esperanza,
que así entretienes mis cansados años,
y en el fiel de los bienes y los daños,
tienes en equilibrio la balanza;
   que siempre suspendida, en la tardanza
de inclinarse, no dejan tus engaños
que lleguen a excederse en los tamaños
la desesperación o confianza:
   ¿quién te ha quitado el nombre de homicida?,
pues lo eres más severa, si se advierte
que suspendes el alma entretenida
   entre la infausta o la felice suerte;
no lo haces tú por conservar la vida
sino por dar más dilatada muerte.[9]

In the octave, the sign and figure, balance and hope, are not directly brought together as an image. She uses the balance to show how she is caught between two conflicting emotions. By always adding a bit of hope to one pan of the balance, the scale is prevented from tipping to the extremes of "desesperación," or suicide. The association of the two parts of the image becomes clearer in the sextet when she presents hope as a cruel assassin. She begins by asking why hope is no longer

   [9] Sor Juana Inés de la Cruz, *Obras completas* (México City: Porrúa, 1972), 137.

called a murderer. This establishes an equivocal correlation between hope and the balance by playing on the slang meaning of "balanza" as a gallows. The conceptual correspondence is worked out on two levels. She provides two reasons for maintaining that hope or optimism is in reality a more cruel assassin. First, like a gallows, it suspends or hangs the soul by entertaining it with false hopes. "Suspender" is a neologism; in Latin it always had the meaning "to hang." Secondly, hope does this not to conserve life, but to give a prolonged death. Of course the two correspondences are based on disparity, since hope is a crueler assassin than the instrument of execution.

Conceived in the tradition of seventeenth-century pessimism, the poem presents life as a suffering—a long drawn-out death. Implicit is the notion that it would be better to end one's life than to extend it with false hope. The intent of the poem to arrive at the unexpected conclusion that hope is an illness and a murderer is achieved through the image of the balance, which first as a scale prolongs a miserable life by not allowing one to fall into despair, and secondly as an implement of execution, gives a long, drawn-out death. The poem achieves its effect more through rhetorical play than through a concentrated existential anguish, and for this reason, the overall effect has an air of playful wit. Even though the basic premises of the poem that life is futile and hope is an assassin are completely pessimistic, the abstract language and concepts give the poem a less bitter effect than Quevedo's pessimistic musings on death and the futility of life.

All three poets, the author of *La Estrella de Sevilla,* Miguel de Barrios, and Sor Juana Inés de la Cruz used the balance as a device for weighing abstract concepts. The next examples rely in part on the visual aspects of the mechanical function of the scale, that as one pan receives more weight and is lowered, the other rises proportionately. This type of image moves completely away from the traditional symbolic meanings of the balance that associated the scales with the Last Judgment or with secular justice. The scale in these images is employed solely for its mechanical properties, and exemplifies what I have called the new direction taken in Golden Age poetry.

Gabriel Bocángel y Unzueta used the image of the balance scale in a poem praising the Congregación del Santo Cristo de la Fe. The poem was well received, for, according to the title, it won first prize. The image of the balance scale praises the piety and religious work of the congregation:

> Y como en peso grave, fiel balanza,
> otro tanto subir hace su opuesta
> quanto ella al centro se profunda y yace.
> De esta noble piedad, surge y renace
> de Dios la Gloria al orbe manifiesta,
> con que se aclamará de gente en gente,
> si infalible no más, más evidente.[10]

The image is simple and clear. The piety and works of the group are weights that lower one arm of the scale and to the same degree raise the other one, which represents the glory of God. Thus, the work of the group, through the weight of its works, exalts God and makes His glory more manifest to the people. The image of the scale is straightforward and relies solely on the observation of the workings of the instrument, freed from traditional symbolic associations.

---

[10] Gabriel Bocángel y Unzueta, *Obras,* I, ed. Rafael Benítez Claros (Madrid: CSIC, 1946), 390-1.

Like Villava's emblem which used the balance to show that Christ's descent into the world exalted man from his fallen position, Lope de Vega conceives of Christ and John the Baptist as pans of a balance scale: as Christ is lowered into humanity, St. John's message becomes truth and raises him to greater glory:

Altas esperanzas
instrumentos tocan,
que hacerle provocan
divinas mudanzas.
Como dos balanzas
se miran los dos,
cuanto baja Dios,
Juan sube hasta verle,
que es primor de su primo
tocarle enfrente.[11]

The last example, also by Lope de Vega, is not only based on the physical properties of the scale, but also includes minute mechanical observations characteristic of metaphysical poetry. In the *comedia de santos El capellán de la Virgen,* San Ildefonso, the seventh-century bishop of Toledo, explains how his modest writings defending the perpetual virginity of María have elevated her to divinity:

Señor, la suma grandeza,
para mostrar su poder,
permite que venga a ser
su defensor mi rudeza,
      para que en esto se entienda,
aunque maravillas raras,
que cosas que son tan claras
basta que yo las defienda.
      Suele un artífice hacer
un peso en tanta igualdad,

---

11 Lope de Vega, *Los pastores de Belén,* 1405b.

que para que la verdad
se pueda en él conocer,
    con sólo un grano de trigo
hace bajar la balanza;
mirad qué verdad alcanza,
pues vuelve el peso conmigo,
    porque siéndolo María
de su divina verdad,
el grano de mi humildad
la subió donde él vivía.[12]

He uses the image of a perfectly balanced scale on which
the addition of a single grain of wheat can completely
lower one of the pans, and raise the other. He says
modestly that the truth was so self-evident that even he in
his simplicity could defend it. The device for measuring
this truth is a balance scale so finely made and perfectly
balanced that the slightest weight can unbalance it. His
writings are like a small humble grain of wheat which,
when placed in one pan, serves to turn all the truth to his
side and raise the Virgen to a heavenly dwelling place.
This passage, like the two previous ones, depends on the
physical characteristics of the balance scale, and its
sensitivity suggests a more advanced instrument of the
technological age.

It is probably not coincidental that the last three
images, the ones that move farthest away from the
traditional symbolism of the balance, are embedded in
religious poems. Counterreformation piety allowed, even
advocated, the use of striking comparisons to jolt the
reader from a lethargic indifference to his spiritual state.
Far from the *conceptismo* of Ledesma, these poems
nevertheless wed the ordinary and humble in the guise of
mechanical imagery to the highest of spiritual concepts.

---

[12] Lope de Vega, *El capellán de la Virgen,* in *Obras,* Biblioteca de
autores españoles, vol. 178 (Madrid: Ediciones Atlas, 1965), 311a.

In the world of the spirit, the class distinctions of the secular disappear, and all of God's creation becomes an example of the unique truth of the creator. Quevedo and others would carry this combination of ignoble mechanical and exalted philosophical truths to a more secular sphere to create some of the finest of Spanish metaphysical poetry.

Even though the balance scale is of great antiquity, both as an instrument and as a metaphor in art and literature, it is evident that in seventeenth-century poetry it achieves a new use. More interest is shown in the finer aspects of the workings of the instrument, and these details become the basis of precise metaphors. The balance scale in Spanish Golden Age poetry is proof of a new interest in the concrete and mechanical aspects of poetic imagery that is quite characteristic of metaphysical poetry. Even though the scientific revolution and a full-blown metaphysical school of poetry did not occur in Spain, it is important to see the same type of minute observation and extended metaphors based on mechanical imagery that characterize both the European scientific and poetical movements. The use of this type of poetic imagery is evidence of Spain's participation in more general European currents of thought, in spite of the fact that other factors came to have dominance in Spanish letters.

5. The Geometer's Compass

Donne's comparison of two lovers to the legs of a mechanical drawing compass is often cited as the prototype of metaphysical imagery. Like the balance scale, the actual use of the geometer's compass in poetry shows that it is closely related to traditional ideas. Even in Donne's image, the phrase "makes my circle just," probably evokes the traditional association of the circle as the most perfect of geometrical figures. The use of imagery to reinforce received ideas is one of the ways in which metaphysical poetry uses the concrete image to project abstractions. The fact that the compass can be a precise tool that relates part to whole (center to circumference) and also evokes the idea of perfection only heightens its poetical possibilities.

The fairly extended use of the compass in Spanish Golden Age poetry demonstrates that Spanish intellectuals and poets did participate in a limited way in the scientific movement and the mode of metaphysical poetry in the seventeenth century. The compass in this body of poetry achieves a variety of effects within a wide range of poetic styles, although most examples can be labeled metaphysical. The compass appears in the terse epigrammatic poem, in contexts that rely on the idea of perfection, in the extravagant metaphysical mode of religious poetry, and finally in poems that make of the image a new emblem that has no relationship to received ideas. This wide diversity of poetry has in common not only its use of mechanical imagery, but also the precise way in which it employs that imagery to define an abstract "metaphysical" relationship concerning man's paradoxical existence.

The metaphysical poets were not the first to be fascinated with the compass as an object of allegorical wit. According to the title of a poem by Juan Alvarez Gato (born 1440-1450, died after 1510), the Duke of Alba had used the compass as an emblematic device; the poem, however, does not make clear the meaning given to the emblem.[1] The image was widely diffused in the sixteenth and seventeenth centuries in the publications of the Dutch printer Christopher Plantin, who adopted the image of the compass with the motto "Labore et Constantia" as the logo of his publishing house.[2] The instrument, which accomplishes its work through constancy in the fixed foot and labor in the movable one, illustrated two moral virtues necessary for completing a task. Often placed on the title page or end leaf of Plantin's books, this device was known all over Europe. Covarrubias includes Plantin's symbolic interpretation among the definitions of compass, seemingly dignifying it as an accepted meaning of the word.[3] In spite of its wide diffusion, the compass was not popular in Spanish emblem books.[4]

Even though the compass in literature at times represents rather far-fetched ideas, its use is closely associated with geometrical notions. Its popularity in poetry in the seventeenth century suggestively parallels the beginnings of the intellectual and scientific movement

---

[1] R. Foulché Delbosc, ed., *Cancionero castellano del siglo XV,* I, NBAE, 19 (Madrid: Bailly-Bailliére, 1912), 265a.

[2] Geffrey Whitney, *A Choice of Emblemes,* ed. Henry Green (New York: Benjamin Blom, 1967), plates 7 and 24.

[3] Sebastián de Covarrubias Orozco, *Tesoro de la lengua castellana o española,* ed. Martín de Riquer (Barcelona: S. A. Horta, 1943).

[4] Juan de Borja is the only Spanish emblematist who uses the image of a compass. He sees it as meaning virtue is found in the middle.

that advocated replacing scholastic explanations based on Aristotelian multiple causes with a purely mathematical and quantitative explanation of physical phenomena (Crombie, II, 122ff). The draftsman's tools became more important in a period which relied increasingly on precise mathematics and geometry to explain the physical world. It is not surprising, therefore, that geometrical notions should enter into literature as metaphors or analogies for showing precise relationships.

The compass and the geometry of the circle were also prominent in poetry because the circle was a traditional symbol for perfection:

> More completely than any other symbol in the universe, the Great Geometer had shown the intricate relationship of the three worlds in the repetition of the Circle of Perfection, which He alone transcended....[5]

Manuel Morales Borrero in his study *Geometría mística del alma* shows that the imagery of the circle, point and sphere were important symbols of the soul, the creator and perfection in religious poetry of the Golden Age. The imagery studied in this chapter differs from the geometrical symbol in that it includes the drawing instrument and is often divorced completely from the traditional symbolism of the perfection of the circle. This symbolism is so often taken for granted that it is difficult to find it stated explicitly. A geometric emblem by Francisco de Villava, titled "Del perfecto," shows an equilateral triangle resting tip down on the top of a circle. He explains that the triangle according to "magos" was a symbol of God and that the circle is justly dedicated to the perfected person:

---

[5] Marjorie Hope Nicolson, *The Breaking of the Circle* (New York: Columbia University Press, 1965), 47.

> ...con razón al perfecto se le da el círculo que es la más
> perfecta de las figuras, la cual le forma saliendo el compás de
> un punto y volviendo al mesmo punto para significar que
> siendo Dios el alfa y omega, principio y fin de las cosas,
> cuando al hombre que salió de Dios por la creación, se
> volviere a Dios por gracia y gloria, será de todo punto
> perfecto....(20v)

The translations by Francisco de la Torre y Sevil of
the Neo-Latin epigrams of John Owen seem to present a
rather mechanical application of these ideas, but actually
the poems achieve their effect by using the imagery to
evoke a series of archetypal ideas rather than creating
complex poetic texture. The geometric metaphor is
perfectly suited to the concise elliptical style of the
epigram, and it is probable that these short paradoxically
phrased poems were instrumental in the development of
the terse metaphysical style. Two of Owen's epigrams
deal with the geometry of the circle. In the first, he draws
a contradiction between the form of the circle and man's
salvation:

DEL CENTRO A LA CIRCUNFERENCIA

No al círculo desde el centro
conduce una línea misma;
y al cielo desde la tierra
un solo camino es vía. (15)[6]

The image, even though paradoxical, is quite simple.
The point represents the earth, or man's existence, and
the Heavens are a sphere circling that point. The
conceptual correspondence is based on a paradox. In
contrast to the circle which has many radii, the Heavens,
represented by the symbolic circle of perfection, have

---

6 Juan Oven, *Agudezas. Segunda parte,* trans. Francisco de la Torre [y
Sevil] (Madrid: Antonio González de Reyes, 1682).

only one way of access. Francisco de la Torre y Sevil, more interested in manifest truths than the convoluted paradoxes of Owen, wrote another epigram inspired by this one: "Adición a Jesús, que es verdadero camino...." He omits the image of the circle and bases his poem on the unstated archetype of Owen's *agudeza,* the Evangelical phrase of the one true way.

In another epigram, Owen used the point and the circle to represent the paradoxical nature of the grandeur of God's manifestations contrasted with His essential unity:

SI LA UNIDAD ARISMETICA
CORRESPONDE AL PUNTO GEOMETRICO

> Más que un punto es Dios inmenso,
> y Dios solo no es más que uno:
> he aquí la inmensa distancia
> entre la unidad y el punto. (124-5)

The translation brings out the "agudeza" even more strongly than the original by directly contrasting the concept of unity with the physical point, suggesting how God far exceeds our basic conception of unity, paradoxically existing as unified point and immensity at the same time.

The translator again added an epigram of his own to clarify the basis of the imagery:

ADICION: COMPAS, PUNTO,
LINEAS Y CIRCULO

> Dios es punto inmenso, y uno,
> su providencia compás,
> líneas todo lo criado,
> círculo la eternidad. (125)

Unlike Owen's epigram, which plays on one of the paradoxes of Christian dogma, the necessary unity of the Godhead contrasted with the immensity and diversity of His creations, Francisco de la Torre y Sevil's poem is a straightforward series of four concise comparisons that explain God and His creation in geometrical relationships. As in Owen's epigram, God is a unified point which is linked to His creation by a compass and the radii that reach back to the creator. The circle appropriately represents eternity, for like the *ouroboros,* the symbol of the snake that devours its own tail, all time turns back on itself in an eternal world, the same idea that Lope de Vega expressed with the image of the circle: "que es círculo eterno Dios y en lo que comienza acaba."[7] Torre y Sevil's geometrical comparisons explain the emanations of God as the work of a draftsman.

This sort of poem probably seems trite to most readers, and so it would be did it not achieve its meaning through the vast number of traditional associations that it recalls. This very image was one of the major reasons that made the idea of a heliocentric universe so attractive to Kepler. According to A. C. Crombie, Kepler's scientific investigation was inspired more by a mystical bent than a desire for understanding abstract mechanics:

> Kepler's central metaphysical conception was of the existence from eternity in the mind of God of archetypal ideas, which were reproduced on the one hand in the visible universe and on the other in the human mind. Of these geometry was the archetype of physical creation and was innate in the human mind. (II, 188)

For this reason, he labored to find in the universe visible images of the geometric archetypes, and his meticulous scientific observations were conducted partly to support these beliefs. The heliocentric universe, more so than the geocentric, was an important example of his reasoning:

---

[7] Lope de Vega, *Los pastores de Belén,* 1521a.

> In the *Cosmographic Mystery* he described at length the visible universe as a sign or image of the Trinity, having the most perfect form of the sphere: the Father was represented by the centre, the Son by the outer surface, and the Holy Ghost by the radius having an equality of relationship between centre and surface. In creating the visible universe in accordance with this geometrical symbolism, God placed at the centre a body to represent the Father by its radiation of power and light: this was the sun. (Crombie, II, 188)

The geometric pattern corresponds perfectly to the seventeenth-century way of thinking that turned to mathematical and quantitative explanations of physical phenomena. In addition, this archetype includes many other archetypal, or traditionally symbolic notions: the universe as divine emanation, the perfection of the circle, the identification of God with the sun, the mutability of the world and the fixed prime mover, etc. In the same way, Francisco de la Torre y Sevil's little poem achieves its meanings only through its semantic associations. The poetry and depth of meaning are supplied by the reader's associations, rather than a complexity of expression.

For Spanish poets of the seventeenth century the compass was an important metaphysical image, the point and circle often symbolizing perfection. In her philosophical poem, *Primero sueño,* Sor Juana Inés de la Cruz described the philosophical attributes of creation in geometrical imagery. Her principle symbol in the poem is the pyramid, but in describing the first cause, she conceives of the tip of the pyramid as a compass point for tracing the circular image of perfection:

> que como sube en piramidal punta
> al Cielo la ambiciosa llama ardiente,
> así la humana mente
> su figura trasunta,
> y a la Causa Primera siempre aspira

> —céntrico punto donde recta tira
> la línea, si ya no circunferencia,
> que contiene, infinita, toda esencia—. (191)

She used the image of the circle again in the same poem to portray man's perfection as the highest of God's creations:

> —que para ser señora
> de las demás, no en vano
> la adornó Sabia Poderosa Mano—:
> fin de Sus obras, círculo que cierra
> la Esfera con la tierra,
> última perfección de lo criado
> y última de su Eterno Autor agrado....(196)

The circle in both images is not a physical representation, but a geometrical symbol of perfection. The compass is not mentioned directly, but is evoked in the phrases "céntrico punto," "circunferencia," and "círculo que cierra."

Perfection is implicit in Lope de Vega's imagery of the circle, but the mechanical properties of the compass are an essential part of the comparison. In the play on San Ildefonso, the saint first uses the balance scale to explain how his modest writings on the Virgin have swayed a large body of opinion, and he continues with another metaphysical image. Something tiny can also be like a compass point from which to draw a larger circle and magnify into a perfect whole that which was small:

> ...de un pequeño punto
> forma un círculo un compás,
> y así desde el punto das
> vuelta a este círculo junto.
> Círculo entero es María,
> donde cupo el mismo Dios.[8]

---

8   Lope de Vega, *El capellán de la Virgen,* 311a.

The saint has used the compass as a geometrical tool to enlarge on his thoughts, which started from a small point that seemed insignificant. From this point, he drew the circle representing the perfection of the Virgin. The mechanical image of the compass explains how the saint has transcended earthly limitations and arrived at a conception of spiritual greatness. Lope shows in the use of the commonplace to illustrate the spiritual one of the chief characteristics of metaphysical wit.

In another play, *La burgalesa de Lerma,* Lope relied again on the properties of the compass to express precise physical relationships. In this case the image serves as a connecting link between two distinct entities, joining the celestial and the earthly. In the play Lope appears as Belardo in one of his favorite disguises, that of a gardener. When he proclaims he has resolved to renounce writing, his master reminds him that he has often made that decision, but has yet to stick to it. Belardo claims that this time his mind is set because of a spiritual commitment:

> Ya tengo puesto el compás
> donde vos no presumís;
> dos puntas tiene, y recelo
> que, en llegándole a asentar,
> no habrá más, porque en el suelo
> una tengo de fijar
> y dar con otra en el cielo.[9]

The word *compás* is used equivocally. On first impression, it seems to be a change of step or pace, but with the mention of the two points, it becomes the familiar drawing instrument. The compass, which is as fixed as his resolution, links him to Heaven and the

[9] Lope de Vega, *La burgalesa de Lerma,* in *Obras,* IV, ed. Emilio Cotarelo y Mori (Madrid: RAE, 1917), 64a.

spiritual, signifying a new life which will exclude writing. Of course, if the points are fixed and there are no more than two, he cannot use it as a writing instrument. This image, both as the idea of a step or rhythm and as a geometrical tool linking two distinct regions, expresses Lope's determination to devote himself to spiritual affairs. As in Donne's image, if the voyage is thought of as death, the compass links two elements which cannot be conceived of as having a physical connection. The compass is a mechanical device used to represent a spiritual bond. As such, it is typical of metaphysical imagery in which a commonplace object expresses man's high spiritual aspirations.

Dámaso Alonso carefully delineated four poets in Lope de Vega's work.[10] Those four figures are in reality only the tip of the iceberg, since Lope's skills included writing in any style he chose. A possible fifth poet is seen in the following poem, written in the *conceptista* style of Alonso de Ledesma. It contains a striking use of the image of the compass:

> Cristo mío, oid mi canto,
> pues os canto con el canto
> que en soledad aprendí.
>   En dos puntos, sol y mi,
> se encierra el canto, mi Dios;
> el sol que canto sois vos,
> yo soy el mí, y el compás
> este canto, que es quien más
> nos ha juntado a los dos.[11]

In reality, the basic metaphor is a musical one, and the

---

[10] Dámaso Alonso, *Poesía española* (Madrid: Editorial Gredos, 1971), 419-493.

[11] Lope de Vega, *El cardenal de Belén,* 220. There is a similar poem in *Los pastores de Belén,* pp. 1493-5. The novel was finished in October, 1611. The autograph ms. of the play is dated August 27, 1610.

other images are based on extravagant conceits of the sort that nearly all ages since have condemned as one of the excesses of Baroque bad taste. This type of metaphysical poem usually has been classified as relying on false wit because the comparisons lack conceptual correspondences and do not reveal important truths about the elements compared. The scene is a favorite subject in seventeenth-century art and poetry: the penitence of Saint Jerome. The stage direction describes the basic iconography familiar from the numerous paintings and sculptures: "Véase San Jerónimo en lo alto, abierto el pecho de la túnica, con un canto en la mano, y un Cristo en una peña." The iconography of the scene is based on a conceit. Saint Jerome was considered to have been hard of heart, as seen in the biting tone of his letters, and only by mollifying his heart with a stone in penitence was he able to achieve his salvation. Adrián de Prado presented the conceit in this way: "Señor, si tuve como piedra el pecho, / con esta piedra ya, sin darle alivio, / carne lo hago por sacar más medra."[12]

Lope uses the word "canto" instead of "piedra," which allows him to introduce the musical image. The accidental correlation is based on an equivoque whose prominence tends to overshadow the correspondence. The song begins as a prayer. Since the "canto" is the stone in his hand, one also begins to imagine how it is supposed to be heard, perhaps as the sound of blows on the chest. Thus, his penitence itself becomes a hymn to God—his self-torture a song in God's praise. Lope continues to develop the image by introducing more equivoques. The song consists of two musical notes (puntos), "sol" and "mi," which he identifies as God

[12] Adrián de Prado, *Canción Real a San Jerónimo en Siria,* in Arthur Terry, *An Anthology of Spanish Poetry,* II (Oxford: Pergamon Press, 1968), 147.

and himself. The correlation "Dios = Sol" is based on an equivoque in which "sol" is the musical note G and an archetypal association of God to the sun, and the correlation "mĭyo" is an equivoque in which "mi" is the musical note E. The rhythm of the music (compás) is the "canto" (stone and song) as well as the blows of the stone that unites the two notes, i.e., the penitent, the humble "mi" and his God, portrayed as "sol," the most eminent and lustrous force of nature. The very act of penance creates a divine harmony that joins man and his maker in a cosmic music.

The two notes, as "puntos," allow yet a further word play and another image. The "puntos" are two points that are joined by a compass, and this instrument unites the penitent and his God in an integral relationship. This compass is the third level of metaphorical meaning to arise from this passage. First the "canto" suggests music, and the effects of the music are spelled out by conceits on the terms of musical imagery. The musical terms introduce both the second image, God and man as cosmic entities, and in the third image, the geometer's compass, the "puntos" are both notes and drawing points and "compás" is both rhythm and a drawing instrument with two legs. As in other compass images, the two legs join elements that would not be united otherwise. The "canto" is first a stone and through successive transformations becomes the rhythm of the blows and a song of two notes. Both music as a harmony and geometry as a relationship serve as metaphors for Saint Jerome's severe penitence which will place him in a harmonic and spatial relationship with the divinity.

Lope's short poem is indeed a *tour de force.* Even though the deep conceptual analysis of the wit shows the appropriateness of the word plays and the profundity of the correspondences established, the poem still leaves the reader dissatisfied. The disparity of the elements related and the falseness of the word plays are disquieting and tend to condemn this poem in spite of the admiration one experiences in the presence of its virtuosity.

Another way in which the compass can be used in metaphysical poetry is to extract an abstract idea from the essence of its function without reference to the traditional ideas of the perfection of the circle. Two metaphysical poets, Francisco López de Zárate and Francisco de Quevedo, take from the operation of the compass lessons on the paradoxical dilemma of man's existence: the desire for fame on the one hand, and on the other, the dangers of extending oneself and seeking fame.

Francisco López de Zárate's sonnet is more traditionally stoic in its ideas and more openly didactic. The circle and point become emblems of the paradox of man's existence: his desire for greatness and his innate limitations:

ENSEÑANDO CON LA ESFERA LA RECTITUD

¡Qué lejos, que por círculo camina,
cuán remoto del punto el que se afana
en los anhelos de la pompa humana,
que en lo más dilatado se termina!
        El grande, el recto, de mayor declina,
no, no sólo declina, se profana
si a exaltación no atiende soberana,
firmamento seguro de ruina:
        Allá, allá te apresura; que el deseo
que repara, y no aspira a lo que espera,
funda dificultades a su empleo,
        recta, como la línea, carrera
nos lleva a lo constante del trofeo:
sólo es descanso el centro de la esfera.[13]

---

[13] Francisco López de Zárate, *Obras varias,* II, ed. José Simón Díaz (Madrid: CSIC, 1947), 260.

The title announces the paradoxical nature of the image. The poet will use the circle to teach uprightness or straightness. The juxtaposition of the curve and straight line underline the paradoxical message of the sonnet. In the image, the circle and point are signs whose figures are abstract and obliquely defined. The point seems to be one's true centerpoint, and the circumference seems to represent a striving for greatness, more specifically defined as "los anhelos de la pompa humana." Each of the quatrains presents a contrary element of the paradox. In the first, the poet makes clear that the person who extends himself in the trials of pomp and honors is the one who finishes exhausted furthest from the center point of his existence. On the other hand, the second quatrain makes clear that great people must participate in their own self-aggrandizement; if not, they are humiliated, in spite of the fact that exaltation is nothing but a sure basis for ruin. The octave establishes the basic paradox: striving to be great distances one from the center of existence, but on the contrary one must pursue such ends to achieve greatness and uprightness.

The first tercet restates the trials of living on the circumference, saying one is pressured, but he adds, one must find a solution, for seeing and criticizing self-aggrandizement in others does not solve the problem, one must have his own way to seek rectitude. Lines 9 and 10 provide examples of the harsh sounds created in the metaphysical style. These two lines play on the endings "-ura," "-para," "-pira," and "-pera," and line 10 sets up a particular dissonance on "aspira" and "espera."

The last tercet provides the solution to the paradox. Rectitude is found in the image itself—in the straight line leading from the circumference to the center point, which as in Plantin's logo, is stable and constant. The imagery itself teaches the message: no matter how exalted one becomes, he will lack a foundation for greatness if he does not show uprightness and rectitude by returning to the center of his real existence, repesented by the point of the circle. Rectitude is found in the straight line of the radius. He reserves the image of straightness until the very end, playing on the paradox of the point and circle, and finally finding the message in the image itself.

Like the epigrams of Owen and Torre y Sevil, the imagery here is abstract and it is difficult to follow the poet's reasoning and the development of his ideas. Also, he uses the signs of the geometrical circle as figures for abstract qualities instead of more concrete, and hence, more accessible figures. Another reason for the difficulty of the poem is that the poet has divorced his imagery from archetypal associations, requiring it to be interpreted on its own terms.

The same paradoxical emblem of the circle is the basis of a remarkable use of the compass in one of Quevedo's metaphysical sonnets:

> ¡Fue sueño ayer; mañana será tierra!
> ¡Poco antes, nada; y poco después, humo!
> ¡Y destino ambiciones, y presumo—
> apenas punto al cerco que me cierra!
>
> Breve combate de importuna guerra,
> en mi defensa, soy peligro sumo;
> y mientras con mis armas me consumo,
> menos me hospeda el cuerpo, que me entierra.
>
> Ya no es ayer; mañana no ha llegado;
> hoy pasa, y es, y fue, con movimiento
> que a la muerte me lleva despeñado.
>
> Azadas son la hora y el momento
> que, a jornal de mi pena y mi cuidado,
> cavan en mi vivir mi monumento. (5)

This sonnet has never been fully explicated. González de Salas titled the poem: "Signíficase la propria brevedad de

81

la vida, sin pensar, y con padecer, salteada de la muerte." Usually a very perspicacious interpreter of Quevedo, he seems to have based his title on the first two lines and the tercets, and he was, therefore, somewhat misled by his partial reading. Modern critics have quoted the first two lines and the tercets as examples of Quevedo's attitude towards the brevity of life,[14] but the central part of the poem in which Quevedo develops a much more subtle paradox of man's existence is usually ignored. As I hope to show, the image of the compass that he introduces in these lines is indeed a worthy competitor of Donne's famous image.

The first two lines of the sonnet place pessimistic limits on the duration of life, typical of the poetry of *desengaño*. Once he has established as a premise the traditional image of life as a mere day, he continues in the next two lines to marvel that within the constraints of such severe limits he should try to achieve something, to carve out a lasting reputation for himself. These two lines have been problematical. Blecua annotated "punto" as meaning "instante"; whereas Price conceived of it as a "full-stop, end." Price commented: "This line seems to mean: 'I scarcely presume that there is an end to this life, which is a siege closing me in.'"[15] He paraphrased Blecua's interpretation as "I presume this siege to have been of hardly an instant's duration." My reading of the line disagrees with both of these interpretations. I read "presumo" not as a transitive verb meaning "to think, to hold an opinion," but as an intransitive verb meaning "to hold an inflated opinion of oneself, to be conceited."

---

[14] Kelley, 47, 158, and Charles Marcilly, "La angustia del tiempo y de la muerte en Quevedo," in Gonzalo Sobejano, ed., *Francisco de Quevedo* (Madrid: Taurus, 1978), 77, 83.

[15] R. M. Price, *An Anthology of Quevedo's Poetry* (Manchester: Manchester University Press, 1969), 86.

"Destino ambiciones" and "presumo" are therefore parallel in construction and complimentary in meaning. The whole next line refers to the subject "yo" which is not stated. For this reason, I have added a dash to Blecua's otherwise excellent punctuation. A paraphrase of my interpretation would be: "¡y [yo]—apenas punto al círculo que me encierra—presumo!", or in English: "and I—barely a point for the circle that surrounds me—dare to presume!" The exclamation marks, indicating the irony of this statement, are absolutely necessary.

The "punto" and "cerco" are in reality part of a compass image which Quevedo uses to express magnificently the paradox of the apparent insignificance and greatness of human existence. He envisions his life as a mere point, but as one from which to project his ambitions. In spite of being an inconsequential jot in the flow of time, the point becomes a sufficiently significant base from which to draw a circle. This image serves perfectly to express the metaphysical paradox of the dignity and misery of man's existence. Man is barely a point in the scheme of the universe, and yet as a point, he can with a compass trace a larger arena of significance about his being.

Typical of seventeenth-century disillusionment, the circle of man's influence extends into a hostile, menacing world. The word Quevedo uses for circle also means a siege, and with the image of the circle both enclosing and besieging him, he introduces war imagery. His existence as a person is a point from which to trace his ambitions, to seek glory, and yet at the same time, this struggle activates the hostility of the world which forms a menacing battle line about the center point of his existence.

The next quatrain continues to develop the paradox of man's insignificance and importance, stressing that one's very attempts to make something out of his life consume that life. The struggle of the individual is one short battle in all of mankind's futile struggle to transcend mortality. The poet as a warrior defending himself is his own worst enemy. His zealous pursuit of lasting fame only shortens his life by exhausting him. The desire and effort needed to extend his life through fame hasten the end of that life; the attempt to extend life on one plane by transcending mortality through fame paradoxically results in mortality and the shortening of life itself. As he uses up his physical forces to achieve fame, his body becomes less a host for the spirit and more of a tomb. Being earth, it begins to bury the spirit, preventing the achievements of which he dreams.

The first tercet returns to the theme of the brevity of life, repeating with greater immediacy the message of the first two lines. The rhythm of these lines, with their short, fast-moving phrases, admirably sums up the speed with which one seems to hasten towards death. The forceful repetition of this theme casts a further pessimistic gloom about man's abilities to achieve fame.

The last tercet concludes summarizing the paradox of mortality and the desire for fame. In one of his most famous images, time becomes the spades, which as a daily wage for man's worries and cares, dig from his being his funeral monument. The comparison is based on an antithesis since there is no possible similarity between time and spades. The image has to be understood on its conceptual level. Time and spades have the same function: they prepare a monument, not just a tomb, which, because it is a monument, is a symbol of the poet's fame. Time itself constructs the monument, excavating it from his "vivir," and receives payment in worry and care. The achievement of fame, which is man's only defense against his mortal condition, serves only to weaken his condition and hasten his mortality. The image of the compass contained the seeds that were developed in the rest of the poem. The tiny point, as it attempts to create a larger space around itself, draws battle lines and creates a circle of hostility that will eventually destroy it. The struggle for earthly immortality is a battle that exhausts the body and paradoxically assures mortality.

The final image recalls Plantin's device with the motto "Labore et Constantia." The constant labor of the workers slowly erodes man's capacities. One very elaborate rendition of Plantin's emblem personifies the two virtues, labor as a day-laborer with a shovel and constancy as a faithful woman (Whitney, 1967: 231). It is of course possible that Quevedo knew this engraving, for the poem contains both the images of the compass and the worker.

Quevedo does not simply present metaphors and conceits expressing the shortness of life, as he does in his other metaphysical sonnets, nor does he moralize on how one must turn to the spiritual to give meaning to life, as he and other writers do in their descriptions of the vanity of the world. Unlike the tenor of his prose writings, which assume a didactic stance, the tone of this sonnet is surprisingly matter-of-fact.[16] Here he presents the very real paradox that even though one's life may seem futile because of its shortness, it is, within the framework of earthly existence, the only thing that has significance. The poet's desire to trace out his ambitions and transcend the limitations of existence on a secular plane assumes a

---

[16] Elsewhere Blecua annotates this poem with passages from Quevedo's prose. The differences are striking. Francisco de Quevedo, *Poemas escogidos,* ed. J. M. Blecua (Madrid: Clásicos Castalia, 1972), 53.

frank importance in this poem that is seldom seen in works arising in the pervasive spiritual mentality of seventeenth-century Spain.

So unlike the naturally poetic rose, the mechanical and scientific compass, with the precise geometrical analogies it draws, is perfect for expressing the matter-of-fact realistic attitude of the metaphysical poet. The compass serves as a link between contrary elements, relating man's existence to the circle, a symbol of perfection, but a symbol whose perfect form can only be assured by the earthly mechanical instrument. In the hands of Lope, López de Zárate and Quevedo, the compass is an image through which mortal man is able to draw the circle of perfection, one in which mere man can extend himself to achievements beyond the limits of his existence, and can relate to the perfection of the universe, but precisely because it is a mere tool, it in turn serves to remind him of his very real limitations.

6. The Mariner's Compass

Since the navigational compass is the most scientific of all notions treated by Golden Age poets, its study requires an understanding of Renaissance science. Magnetic forces were the point of departure for the study of all physical forces in nature. Laying at the heart of Spanish Renaissance scientific investigation, navigational science also requires an understanding of the occult because of the lack of a defined boundary between real science and the superstitious occult sciences. As a non-visible force, magnetism serves as a perfect analogy for all unexplained attractions, both in science and poetry.

The discovery and history of magnetism are lost in the uncertainties of unrecorded history. It was known in the ancient world, and Plato, Aristotle, Lucretius, and Pliny, among others, referred to its mysterious forces. Pliny gave an enchanting account of its discovery by a shepherd Magnes who observed that the nails in his shoes stuck to Mount Ida. He also associated magnetism and the diamond, saying the diamond has the power to cancel the force of the magnet. The seventeenth-century Jesuit scholars Juan de Pineda and Johannes Kircher attributed the discovery of the magnet to Solomon.[1]

The development of the magnetic compass occurred some time in the Middle Ages, although the exact period

---

[1] The facts in this and the following paragraphs are summarized from José María Martínez-Hidalgo y Terán, *Historia y leyenda de la aguja magnética. Contribución de los españoles al progreso de la náutica* (Barcelona: Editorial Gustavo Gili, 1946), and López Piñero (1979).

and place of its discovery is unknown. Apparently it was first used in China and transmitted to Europe by Arab scientists. It was known in medieval Europe, being mentioned by an Icelandic poet in the twelfth century and described by Alexander Neckham around 1180. In the primitive compass, the magnetized metal was placed in a hollow cane or cork and floated on water; later was it mounted on a spindle and superimposed upon a windrose to produce the modern compass indicating the cardinal directions. The compass was prevalent in the Mediterranean in the late Middle Ages. Because of the practical experience gained through their numerous exploratory and merchant voyages, Spaniards played an important role in the development of the compass and other navigational instruments in the sixteenth century. López Piñero summarizes the Spanish scientific contributions in the Renaissance: "En su mayor parte corresponden a saberes aplicados como la náutica, la ingeniería naval, la cartografía y la ingeniería militar, en las que nuestro país ocupó durante casi un siglo un puesto dirigente" (1969, 16). He calls the Spanish contribution to nautical literature "sin duda una de las principales aportaciones españolas a la literatura científica de la época" (1979, 199). The Spanish treatises were extremely popular in the rest of Europe:

> ...los tratados de Medina y Cortés alcanzaron en Europa una extraordinaria difusión e impusieron la imagen de la nueva disciplina.... El tratado de Medina alcanzó quince ediciones en francés entre 1554 y 1633, cinco en holandés desde 1580 a 1598, tres en italiano (1554, 1555 y 1609) y dos en inglés. El de Cortés, por su parte, tuvo diez ediciones en inglés entre 1561 y 1630. (López Piñero, 1979: 202)

The wide diffusion of these treatises proves the importance the Spaniards achieved in the science of navigation.

They also made important contributions to the understanding of magnetic declination. Since magnetic north does not correspond to true north, the compass points either to the east or west of true north, depending on the longitude. Declination was known in the Middle Ages, but Columbus was the first to observe significant variations of magnetic declination. As he voyaged further to the west than any previous navigator, he was "fascinated by the discovery that it changed from East in the Mediterranean, to zero off the Azores, to West as he proceeded westward across the Atlantic."[2] He had discovered that the degree of declination depended on longitude. In 1551, the Spanish cosmologist, Martín Cortés, offered an explanation for declination, positing a "punto atractivo" whose geographical location differed from true north. Thus, at a location in which both poles were in line, the compass would point to true north, but sailing to the east or west of that point, the compass, still pointing to magnetic north, would decline further and further from true north. López Piñero calls this hypothesis "...un auténtico 'clásico' en la historia de los estudios del magnetismo terrestre" (1979, 206).

The advances made by the Spanish in navigational science are proof of a keen interest in practical questions, but a complete understanding of the poetical uses of the compass requires a knowledge of the place of magnetism in general scientific theories. An interest in magnetic attraction lay at the heart of scientific speculation and investigation by Renaissance scholars, who undertook a concentrated study of the so-called occult forces of nature. Although the modern conception of occult as superstitious stems directly from these Renaissance ideas,

---

[2] Marie Boas, *The Scientific Renaissance. 1450-1630* (New York: Harper Torchbooks, 1962), 192.

the study of hidden properties, whether they were astrological, alchemical, or magical, was a legitimate and respectable effort to understand better the physical sciences, and in most cases, these studies developed into legitimate modern sciences. Marie Boas emphasized the unity of science and pseudo-science in the Renaissance: "...there was no difference between natural philosophy and mystic science; but rather ... men saw that each rational science had its magical, occult or supernatural counterpart. Applied astronomy might be either navigation or astrology; applied chemistry either metallurgy or the search for the Philosophers' stone" (Boas, 167).

Renaissance philosophers called attention to the great number of natural affinities and repulsions in the physical world that could not be explained by the theory of the four elements. This prevailing theory adequately explained certain natural attractions, such as gravity, by asserting that each element had a natural place in the universe. A stone would always seek the center of the earth and fire would always rise. The theory also explained the sympathy and antipathy between the elements, classifying them as humid or dry and cold or hot, and also explained chemical transformations. Fire changes water to steam (air) by transforming its secondary characteristic. Water is primarily humid and secondarily cold. The heat removes the coldness and forms a new element having the properties of heat and humidity, that is, air. Likewise, in medicine, an herb classified as dry (lentils, for example) would serve to cure the congestion (humidity) of a common cold.

Occult forces, however, were hidden properties that could not be explained by the classification of the characteristics of the four elements. The prime example of such a force was the magnet—a stone or metal whose external properties did not differ from those of the iron it attracted. Other forces, more trivial to our way of thinking, were also considered in the same category, such as the hatred of dogs for cats, the attraction of the sunflower to the sun, and magical and astrological forces. Marie Boas maintains that the separation of science and magic only occurred much later than the period studied here: "...sixteenth-century natural magic was indistinguishable from true experimental science in its investigation of the effects of mysterious forces by means of observation and experiment. Natural magic and experimental science finally parted company when the latter was allied to that particular form of natural philosophy known as the mechanical which endeavored to understand both the effects of such mysterious forces, and their cause, in truly rational terms" (Boas, 185). It was believed that the investigation of these forces would reveal sources of power that could be utilized by man: "Underlying the whole is the belief that by observing the sympathies and antipathies associated with natural objects, one can arrive at an understanding of their essential nature and a control of their virtues, since it is by means of the hidden virtues (or forces) of things that apparent wonders are performed" (Boas, 188). In spite of much of the nonsense generated by this activity, it is evident that the discovery of electricity and even atomic energy are simply extensions of the Renaissance belief in occult forces that man can use for great power.

The compass and magnetic forces were the prime examples of the secret sympathies and antipathies in nature. Pero Mexía, a Renaissance scientific popularizer, classified magnetism among the natural sympathies and antipathies. His description of magnetic force is a good summary of a learned man's knowledge on this subject in the sixteenth century:

... pero hay otras propiedades, y virtudes en las cosas que se llaman ocultas y maravillosas, porque no se sabe de donde les vengan, ni se entiende la causa, ni razón. ... Vemos a la piedra imán alzar los pedazos de acero, y clavos del suelo, que pesan casi tanto como ella y la razón escóndenos, y no la sabemos. Aunque bien se conoce, que aquella calidad no es de elementos, no lo causa el calor del fuego, ni la sequedad de la tierra, sino otra fuerza secreta y escondida. Y no solamente tiene la piedra imán esta fuerza, pero comunícala, y préstala, que una punta de cuchillo tocada en la misma piedra recibe, y participa tanto de aquella propiedad, que otro día alza con la misma punta la aguja, o clavo, o cosa de hierro, o acero, y el acero así tocado también toma otra propiedad maravillosa de la misma piedra, que puesto en su libertad, se enderece, pone hacia el polo del mundo, o a otro punto cercano a él. Y de esta manera se hace las agujas de marear, que no sabemos porqué, ni cómo.[3]

Mexía's brief description is carefully written, and reveals a knowledge of several observational and experimental qualities of the magnet. Having first discussed the known properties of the elements: hot, cold, dry, and wet, he begins to give examples of the secret affinities and oppositions between things. The magnet is the prime example of properties that cannot be explained by ordinary classifications. Having placed the discussion within its proper categorical framework, he proceeds to describe the force. He says the magnet has sufficient force to lift weights "que pesan casi tanto como ella." This phrase would indicate an awareness of experiments testing the power of the magnet by weighing the objects lifted. He also adds that the magnet can impart its power to other pieces of iron, and these conserve the force over a period of time. Finally he says the compass "se enderece y pone hacia el polo del mundo," and he allows for magnetic declination by adding the phrase "o a otro

---

[3] Pero Mexía, *Silva de varia lección* (Madrid: Imprenta Real, 1669), 286.

punto cercano a él.'' Even though he does not directly state it, the purpose of these observations was an attempt to understand the power of the magnet and utilize its force. Such an intention lies behind much of seventeenth-century scientific experimentation.

Not only philosophers and natural scientists took an interest in the occult properties of magnetism and the magnetic compass, but poets also saw the secret attractions as perfect for drawing poetic analogies and forming imagery. Several poets show an interest in the observational and theoretical aspects of magnetism. Perhaps it is not accidental that two of these passages occur in pastoral poems. The division established between nature and technology in modern times makes it almost unfathomable to think that the pastoral, the idealistic genre that exalted the purity of nature and the natural life, should have included ''scientific observations.'' Science is, however, a part of nature, and the exaltation of nature could logically include the praise of the ''occult'' forces of nature, no matter how disconcerting it may be to the modern ecologist.

Góngora placed a description of the use of the compass in his *Soledad primera*. The description occurs in the long passage in which the old shepherd condemns navigation. The intent of the condemnation seems more modern than might be supposed from the baroque poetic technique. He attacks navigation as a perverted use of natural goods. The greed of a ''labrador fiero...en mal nacido pino'' had cut down whole forests and sent them to the sea. Within the condemnation of sea-faring is a description of the use of the compass:

> Náutica industria investigó tal piedra,
> que cual abraza yedra
> escollo, el metal ella fulminante
> de que Marte se viste, y lisonjera,

93

solicita el que más brilla diamante
en la nocturna capa de la esfera,
estrella a nuestro Polo más vecina;
 y con virtud no poca,
 distante le revoca,
 elevada la inclina
 ya de la Aurora bella
al rosado balcón, ya a la que sella,
 cerúlea tumba fría,
 las cenizas del día.
En esta pues fiándose atractiva,
del Norte amante dura, alado roble,
no hay tormentoso cabo que no doble,
ni isla hoy a su vuelo fugitiva.[4]

The description of the compass, however, does not suggest a condemnation of sea-faring. In it, the poet strives to be as detailed and scientifically correct as possible. Nieremberg cited this passage in his *Curiosa Philosophia,* paying tribute to Góngora's erudition: "no le ignoró el Pindaro Español don Luis de Góngora en la que de esta piedra con comprensión cantó."[5] Góngora first says the magnet is attracted to iron, "el metal...fulminante / de que Marte se viste," as ivy clings to a cliff. The comparison with clinging ivy serves to classify magnetism as a natural occult attraction. The sparks produced by the metal (fulminante) suggests not only danger and war, but also occult properties of fire hidden in the metal. The references to ivy and sparks establish from the beginning the theoretical context of sympathy and antipathy.

The obedient magnet is attracted to the brightest star in the northern sphere of the Heavens—the star nearest the north pole. The qualification "más vecina" suggests

---

 [4] Luis de Góngora, *Obras completas* (Madrid: Aguilar, 1961), 644.

 [5] Juan Eusebio Nieremberg, *Curiosa philosophia y tesoro de las maravillas de la naturaleza* (Madrid: Imprenta del Reyno, 1639), 365.

Martín Cortés's explanation of declination, that is, that true north and magnetic north do not coincide. Góngora says the magnet is attracted to the North Star, which is near, but not precisely over geographic north. The star attracts the compass, inclining it either slightly to the east or to the west, the verb *inclinar* suggesting declination. This passage has generally been imperfectly understood because it is unclear whether the referent of "elevada" is the "piedra" or the "estrella." In their published commentaries, Salcedo Coronel and Pellicer interpreted it according to a theory in Gilbert's *De magnete* (1600), which stated that as the compass approached true north, it would begin to spin.[6] While it is noteworthy that the two commentators knew Gilbert's treatise, it is obvious that they misinterpreted the passage. "Elevada" does not refer to the ship or the "piedra imán" sailing north, but to the star in the northern sky. The *Diccionario de Autoridades* gives four distinct astronomical definitions for "elevado." The one that seems to fit is "se dice...por tener mayor latitud boreal," that is to say, higher in the northern sky, of which the North Star would be the highest. Since modern editions base their commentaries on those of Salcedo Coronel and Pellicer, it is easy to explain the survival of the misinterpretation.

Góngora concludes the passage adding that the compass has made possible navigation in difficult seas and to remote places. Behind the elegance of the High

---

[6] Luis de Góngora, *Soledades. Comentadas por D. Garcia de Salcedo Coronel* (Madrid: Imprenta Real, n.d.), 79v-81r, and Joseph Pellicer de Salas y Tovar, *Lecciones solemnes a las obras de Don Luis de Gongora y Argote* (Madrid, 1630; fsml. rpt. New York: Georg Olms, 1971), 432-445. The earlier unpublished commentary of Manuel Ponce employs the same ambiguity as Góngora's original. Dámaso Alonso, "Manuel Ponce, primer comentarista de Góngora", in *Libro-homenaje a Antonio Pérez Gómez,* I (Cieza: La fonte que mana y corre, 1978), 10.

Baroque style with its hyperbata and numerous mythological references is a carefully presented exposition of magnetic forces and the use of the compass, including presentation of a correct theoretical context and a description and explanation of magnetic declination. The scientific precision of this presentation and the lack of an underlying metaphorical meaning make it unique among the examples cited in this chapter. The interest in a purely scientific description corresponds to the Baroque ideal of making poetry useful by the inclusion of erudition and moral teachings.[7]

The next two examples, even though metaphorical, show an interest in the experimental aspects of magnetism. Lope de Vega uses one of the visible effects of magnetism as a simple metaphor for describing one's hair rising with fear:

> Porque vi mis cabellos esparcidos,
> como al espín las medio blancas puntas,
> y mi amor y deseo arrepentidos.
>   Así menuda arena (si la juntas
> la imán debajo de un papel) se eriza.[8]

In the larger context, Tirsi is recounting an apparition called forth by magic. The sight of it made his hair stand on end, like the quills on a porcupine, or like iron filings on a piece of paper when a magnet is passed under them. The comparison is not integral, but does add a vivid description of his fear. It shows a curiosity in magnetism and an elementary experiment showing that the force of the magnet can pass through neutral objects, such as paper. Perhaps Lope was also suggesting a comparison

---

[7] Luis Carrillo y Sotomayor, *Libro de la erudición poética,* ed. Manuel Cardenal Iracheta (Madrid: CSIC, 1946).

[8] Lope de Vega, *Obra poética,* 179-180.

between magical correspondences (which make the spirits come forth or the hair rise) and the secret sympathies between the magnet and filings. Along with the interest in observational details, the full context of the image suggests that it still has not lost its association with magic and superstition.

Another simple experiment with magnetism is seen in an image by Calderón: "sin ver si vivo o si muero, / estaré como el acero / suspenso entre dos imanes."[9] The image of a piece of steel suspended in the magnetic fields between two magnets, each of which is capable of overpowering the other and bringing the steel into contact with itself, serves as a sign describing the indecision of a character held between two powerful passions, either one of which is capable of dominating and destroying him. Calderón uses the image of scientific attraction to present in visual terms the dilemma of a person drawn by two powerful desires.

The invisible forces of magnetic attraction became something of a cliché among Baroque writers, who abused the word "norte" as a common expression for goal or end. In poetry, magnetism most often served as a metaphor for the physical attraction between man and woman, as in the following quatrain of a sonnet by Sor Juana Inés de la Cruz:

> Si al imán de tus gracias atractivo
> sirve mi pecho de obediente acero,
> ¿para qué me enamoras lisonjero,
> si has de burlarme luego fugitivo? (137)

In Rojas Zorrilla's *Del rey abajo, ninguno,* doña Blanca uses magnetism as an image for the force of her love:

---

[9] Pedro Calderón de la Barca, *Obras completas,* II, ed. Angel Valbuena Briones (Madrid: Aguilar, 1960), 222a.

No quieren más las flores al rocío,
que en los fragantes vasos el sol bebe;
las arboledas la deshecha nieve,
que es cima de cristal y despúes río;
    el índice de piedra al norte frío,
el caminante al iris cuando llueve,
la obscura noche la traición aleve,
más que te quiero, dulce esposo mío.

               (*Diez comedias,* 713)

The Renaissance theories of natural affinities are apparent in this passage. The "imán" occurs in the context of secret sympathies to which she compares her love. Through these comparisons, she declares her love, even though invisible, to be as real as other unseen attractions in the universe.

Calderón develops further the context of occult sympathies for both the magnet and the compass in *Casa con dos puertas mala es de guardar.* In the opening scene, Marcela orders Lisardo to stop following her. He replies citing three examples of natural affinities:

    Difícilmente pudiera
conseguir, señora, el sol
que la flor del girasol
su resplandor no siguiera;
difícilmente quisiera
el norte, fija luz clara,
que el imán no le mirara;
y el imán difícilmente
intentara que obediente
el acero le dejara.
    Si el sol es vuestro esplendor,
girasol la dicha mía;
si norte vuestra porfía,
piedra imán es mi dolor;
si es imán vuestro rigor,
acero mi ardor severo;
pues ¿cómo quedarme espero,
cuando veo que se van

98

mi sol, mi norte y mi imán,
siendo flor, piedra y acero? (II, 276)

The sun cannot prevent the sunflower from following it, nor the north star stop the compass, nor can the magnet stop iron from being attracted to it. These three secret sympathies are compared to the lover's happiness, pain, and passion, all of which find their corresponding attraction in the object of his desire. It is useless for the mistress to reject him, for he is inevitably attracted to her. The typical Calderonian repetition summarizes the previous images, giving emphasis to the points of attraction. These three comparisons achieve their meaning within the theoretical context of natural sympathies and antipathies.

Delitalá y Castelví and Quevedo also compare love to the occult forces of nature, but both include astral influences among the mysterious sympathetic forces. Delitalá y Castelví presents the forces of love as a grand master scheme of the cosmos, comparing secret affinities and causes to the implacable force of love that controls his life:

¡Ha del amor!, sagrada Astrología,
que predomina en cuerpos sublunares
sin excepción de tierras y de mares,
por dilatador, términos del día.

¿Qué respecto?, ¿qué imán?, ¿qué simpatía
es ésta, cielos, con que en sus altares
sacrificios votamos singulares,
engañada la propia fantasía?

Con un impulso arrastra soberano
al arbitrio más libre y alterano,
máximas ejerciendo de tirano.

¿Por qué razón, o celestial clavero,
me sujetas a imperios de su mano,
haciéndome vivir de lo que muero?[10]

---

[10] Joseph Delitalá y Castelví, *Cima del Monte Parnaso* (Caller: Onofrio Martin, 1672), 123.

Placed first among his love lyrics, it begins with a bold apostrophe crying out to love and comparing it to astral influences that govern everything below the first sphere of Heaven. These forces, like the force of love, control the land and seas, and even the length of the day. This comparison parallels on a profane level the scholastic principle that God's constant love sustains the natural world which would cease to exist without His continual care and attention. For Delitalá y Castelví it is the profane Cupid who controls and dominates. In the second quatrain, the poet characterizes the forces of love, borrowing terminology from feudalism (respecto) and science (imán, simpatía), and developing a comparison with religion. The first tercet develops the idea of a secular lord (tirano) who dominates even the freest of spirits, issuing the cruelest laws (máximas). In a final play of concepts, he queries why love makes him live by suffering.

As a metaphysical poet, or even as a poet, Delitalá y Castelví cannot compete with Quevedo. The opening apostrophe is striking and exciting, but the final play on "vivir" and "morir" is very weak and hackneyed. If the last line were as exciting as the first, the poem would indeed have achieved success, for the development of the ideas is skillfully carried out. The comparisons, based on archetypes, of love to a false god and to a tyrant, even though overworked in the courtly love tradition, are given new meaning and executed with a degree of freshness. The force of love is the subject of the poem, and besides being characterized as a god and tyrant, it is compared to astral influences which incline the will of man. These in turn are placed in their proper scientific context as a type of magnetism and occult attraction. The world is a series of secret sympathies between objects, love the one between man and woman. The poet elevates profane love to the level of a cosmic force controlling the will of man in the same way secret forces control and govern the physical world.

Quevedo develops a sonnet based on the image of the compass as the teacher of an absent lover. He presents various aspects of the compass, exploiting each one to make a point about love and its relationship to human emotion:

AMANTE AUSENTE ESCOGE POR MAESTRO DE SU AMOR LA PIEDRA IMAN

Esta, que duramente enamorada,
piedra desde la tierra galantea
al Norte, que en el cielo señorea
con fija luz la redondez sagrada;
    ésta que sabe amar tan apartada,
maestro de mi amor ausente sea;
y al éxtasi que tiene por tarea,
imite l'alma en astros abrasada.
    Y pues sabe del Ponto en la llanura
diferenciar las sendas, y del viento
regula en breve cerco la locura,
    enseñe a navegar mi pensamiento;
porque de la atención a su luz pura
no le aparten suspiros ni lamento. (48-9)

The title announces the traditional courtly love theme of the absent lover, the compass serving as an example of how the lover should remain faithful. In the first two lines, he uses the violent hyperbaton of "esta" and "piedra" to represent graphically the separation of the lover from his mistress, and how their relationship will continue to exist even though physically separated. The adverb "duramente" is a pun on the hardness of the stone and the fixedness of the attraction. The compass loves the North Star, the verb "galantear" characterizing the vacillating needle as it seeks its point of attraction, the North Star, which governs the perfect sphere of the heavens with its steady light.

101

The second quatrain establishes a series of images based on the movement of the compass. Always seeking the same point, the compass is a sign for the lover dominated by his mistress. For this reason he hopes the compass will be his teacher in love because it knows how to love from a distance. The vacillations of the wobbly needle are a sign for the soul writhing in ecstasy, and he hopes his soul will imitate it. In both these images, the movement of the compass provides a similitude for an exemplary aspect of love, which establishes its authority as a teacher. The accidental correlation in the image of the "astros" is based on the archetypal cliche which saw in the mistress's eyes the beauty of the stars. On the level of the conceptual correspondence they suggest astral influences which determine the course of love and govern the lover's will. And finally, the soul controlled by these astral influences, be they stars or eyes, recalls the magnet subject to the forces of the North Star. This is an "agudeza por proporción," according to Gracián's system of classification. As the magnet is to the North Star, so let the soul be to astral influences. The fact that lovers traditionally blamed their uncontrollable passions on astral influences and equated their mistress's eyes with the stars, claiming the eyes had mysterious bewitching powers, provides multiple lines of correspondence and makes the comparison more ingenious and apt. The secret sympathy between the magnet and the North Star is a metaphor for the way the poet conceives his love, a mysterious attraction which controls and directs his attention. Unlike the comparisons of Sor Juana Inés de la Cruz and Rojas Zorrilla, Quevedo not only presents the simple metaphor, but also exploits each aspect of it.

In the sextet, he concludes the extended comparison by erecting an elaborate image. Since the magnet can find its way in unmarked courses and is unaffected by winds, he imagines it as measuring and controlling the wild wind within its small case; "cerco" of course gives the idea of having fenced in the winds. The correlation to the lover comes from the phrase "la locura del viento," which recalls his passion. The correspondence makes the point that in the absence of the beloved the unstable wind could take a new direction. Since the compass is free from and actually dominates such fickle influences and loves steadfastly, he asks it to instruct his thought in the art of navigation, and direct it to the beloved—to the one pure light—and not let it be distracted by passions, or winds, such as sighing and laments. Again, the star with its fixed and pure light is the object of attraction. He hopes it will inform and guide his thought, overcoming distracting self-pitying sentiment. As often in the poetry of Quevedo, the idealism of pure Platonic love is played off against another system of love, usually sensual love. In this case, however, he hopes an idealistic love can overcome the weeping and self-pity characteristic of the courtly and Petrarchan lovers. The compass attracted to the "fija luz" of the dominating North Star should be an example to the lover when absent from his beloved. Instead of falling into self-pity and despair—one recalls numerous sonnets and shepherd's laments from earlier poetry—, he hopes he will remain faithful to his one pure love, by avoiding sensual self-pitying emotions. The last words suggest that Petrarchan love, which repressed and overcame the sensuality of physical love, actually fell into another trap of sensuality which could only be overcome by rejoicing ("tiene por tarea el éxtasi") in the purity of a constant reciprocal love.

Typical of the type of metaphysical poem that develops through concrete imagery one extended comparison, this sonnet exploits each aspect of the image. The hyperbaton suggests the separation of the lovers. The hardness of the stone and its fixed direction are the bases of puns. The wobbly needle is first a nervous lover and later the ecstasy of pure love. The fact that it needs no points of reference and is not affected by the wind portrays the lover's fixed purpose and his victory over sensual passion. Traditional metaphors are converted into conceits: "eyes = stars" is the basis of a new comparison showing his attraction. Finally the complete idealism of human love is played off against the imperfection which human passion introduces into love relations. The contrast of extreme idealism and realism is one of the aspects in which Quevedo and Donne correspond most closely. This sonnet is undoubtedly one of the finest metaphysical poems included in this study.

Calderón brilliantly employs the image of the compass at the beginning of *Psalle et sile,* a long meditative poem explaining how the two precepts of the title: sing and guard silence, can be united in one single precept. His definitions play on the antithesis of the title, for "callar" is "muda / prisión del silencio," and "cantar," to the contrary: "no solo es / romperlas, pero entonarlas / al acordado compás / de métrica consonancia" (1).[11] The "compás" is introduced in a reference to the rhythm of the song, but through an equivoque also suggests two other images, the rhythm of the pilgrim's step and the mariner's compass, that he develops in the following stanzas:

> Ignorante peregrino
> soy, que a las piadosas aras
> del Sagrario de María,
> condujo no errante planta,
> fijo norte sí, en aquella
> aguja que sobre tantas

---

[11] Pedro Calderón de la Barca, *Psalle et Sile,* in *Obras menores* (Cieza: La fonte que mana y corre, 1969).

104

cervices, ya de edificios,
ya de montes se levanta
    a ser en el desvelado
eco de sus atalayas,
cada clamor un sonoro
clarín de la fe cristiana,
    de cuyo animado bronce,
aun más que del de su fama
conducido, llegué apenas
al pie de sus torres altas,
    cuando inspirado del mismo
boreal imán de mis ansias,
saludé el umbral, diciendo:
Salve, basílica santa. (1a)

The steps (compás) are those of a pilgrim guided to the Cathedral of Toledo. He has not been guided by his wandering steps, but by the fixed north of the Cathedral itself. In a clever fictive conceit, the "aguja" is both the cathedral spire and the needle of the compass, both the pointer and the point of attraction. The equivoque serves to correlate the two pointers because of the their physical similarity as pointers, but their dissimilarity is seemingly greater. The image works not on a realistic level, but on the level of conceptual correspondence. Both spires serve as pointers to direct him to his goal. A similar image is the "animado bronce" of the ringing bells that guide the pilgrim. If we accept with poetic license a correlation of "bronce" for iron on the basis of their both being metals, then the bells are the compass which is animated and directs him to the north of the cathedral. Inspired by the "boreal imán," the northern magnetic point, in this case the cathedral, which was the goal of his desires, he sings a sonnet of salutation. The sonnet itself does not use the compass image, but it is further developed in the three stanzas that follow the sonnet:

105

Dije, y con temor, tocando
del perdón la primer grada,
(que líneas de perdón nadie
pudo sin temor tocarlas),
    al ámbito pasé, en cuyas
naves la vista engolfada,
sin peligros de tormenta,
corrió achaques de borrasca.
    ¡O cuántas muertas noticias,
vivas memorias! ¡O cuántas!,
ofuscado el pensamiento
revolvió al verse en su estancia. (2)

Elizabeth Boyce has observed that the confusion that the poet feels upon reaching his "boreal imán" is a further extension of the image of the compass, which, when it is directly under the pole, begins to spin.[12] This theory had been announced by Gilbert in 1600, and was known in Spain. Salcedo Coronel had referred to it in his commentaries on Góngora and Nieremberg cites him in his *Curiosa Philosophia*. Calderón could have been familiar with any of these writings. Like Quevedo, Calderón exploits the full possibilities of the image of the compass, using it to represent man's attraction, or unfulfilled desire for union with God. The steadfastness of the compass represents not only man's faith, but also the firm faith of the church, which is always present and guiding him just as the North Star guides the navigator.

Unlike the balance and draftsman's compass, the navigational compass is more clearly related to seventeenth-century scientific activities. Other than a few observational details in some writers, the main use of the compass is, like magical correspondences or astral influences, to serve as an analogy for invisible forces that govern human life, such as human love and love of God.

---

[12] Elizabeth S. Boyce, "Calderón's *Psalle et Sile:* The Meditative Art and the Metaphysical Mode," *Iberoromania* 6 (1980), 122-146.

The information and ideas associated with magnetism and the compass are so vast that a simple reference is sufficient to apply a large body of metaphysical knowledge of invisible forces to a poetic context. For that reason, many references are very short; the simple words "imán" or "norte" often serve as metaphors to evoke many scientific and pseudo-scientific associations. Such is the case with the sonnet of Delitalá y Castelví, which uses the word "imán" to recall the larger context of occult sympathies and astral influences to create a whole cosmos of love. Another way of expanding these comparisons is in the creation of elaborate images based on the properties of the compass, as in the sonnet by Quevedo. The navigational compass can indeed be a powerful poetic metaphor precisely because it represents a real, but unseen, relationship. Quevedo and Calderón exploit these basic ideas in their meditations on the perfection of love, the invisible forces of perfect human love, either for woman or for God.

PART III

Timepieces and the Measurement of Time

7. Concepts of Time in the Pastoral

The preoccupation with time and its symbolical representation in the clock brings us to the crux of Baroque sensibility: an all-consuming concern with the paradoxes of appearance and reality and the search for the absolute in a world buffeted by chance and instability. Warnke finds a preoccupation with the dichotomy between true reality, which is otherworldly and unseen, and the appearance of reality, which is the mutable world about us, as the essential unifying spirit of the Baroque (Warnke, 1972, 22-3). This concern, either expressed emotionally as anguish or intellectually as a series of paradoxes, often lies at the basis of all Baroque artistic expression. The paradoxes, contradictions, and dichotomies that inform Baroque literature can also be seen in general terms as the problem of the one and the many, which Smith posited as the essence of metaphysical poetry (Smith, 1968: 162). The one (reality), which is general, perfect, and unchanging, is in direct contrast to the imperfect world (of appearances) we know, which is individual, multitudinous, and ever changing.

This problem achieves special significance with the conception of time. The need to formulate, as did Plato, the idea of a perfect bed in order to account for the existence of abstractions remains an intellectual problem that is not a source of human anguish, but when the problem of the one and the many, reality or the appearance of reality, is manifested in time, the idea of capturing an ideal moment or of existing in an unchanging immovable eternity is in direct contradiction to the many passing moments that confront man in the earthly progression of time. Man senses and reacts emotionally to the irreversible progression of events that he cannot change and which signify his own personal destruction. Existence as a progression of time and decay has always perturbed mankind, who has found consolation in various concepts of static, never-decaying existence. The problem of the mutability of the world and time is an old question, found in the earliest of literature such as the *Lamentations of Jeremiah* and the pre-Socratic philosophers, especially Heraclitus and Zeno of Elea, who propounded logical paradoxes on the contradictions of permanence and flux.[1]

The accounts of the history of philosophical attitudes towards time are less reliable for Renaissance and Baroque thought than for any other period. Generally, they do not agree among themselves either in their broad outlines or in their details. Most often their conclusions vary according to the particular philosopher examined who is taken as representative of the whole epoch.[2] This is misleading because the Renaissance is a period of

---

[1]   J. T. Fraser, *Of Time, Passion, and Knowledge* (New York: George Braziller, 1975), 4-5; and G. J. Whitrow, *The Natural Philosophy of Time* (Oxford: Clarendon Press, 1980), 190-9.

[2]   J. T. Fraser, 30-35, has the fullest discussion. George Poulet, *Studies in Human Time* (Baltimore: The Johns Hopkins Press, 1956), discusses the philosophies of Montaigne and Descartes. The usual method is to jump from the Middle Ages to Kant, as does J. B. Priestley, *Man and Time* (London: Aldus Books, 1964), 165-6.

greatly conflicting philosophies and of diverse and contradictory currents in literature. Since it is difficult to find agreement among the historians consulted, it seems best for this study to go to some aspect of literature itself and analyze the manifestations of time as a poetical theme. This allows for the best understanding of the poetical response to various concepts of time and also provides a background for understanding the image of the clock in Baroque poetry. Time became a major theme in seventeenth-century lyrical poetry, which treated extensively the theme of the brevity of life.[3] A more complete view, however, of the different concepts of time which concerned Golden Age poets is seen in pastoral poetry. Usually defined as a timeless world, the pastoral actually explores and contrasts various ideas of time, and the study of the pastoral makes it possible to distinguish the following four concepts of time in Golden Age poetry.

Linear Time. Most commonly associated with seventeenth-century lyric poetry is destructive linear time, treated as the theme of the brevity of life. According to Panofsky and Whitrow,[4] this concept was unknown in antiquity and only developed during the Middle Ages. It produced the symbol of Father Time, the grim reaper either as an old man or skeleton with a scythe. These symbols represent destructive time that consumes human existence.

Cyclical Time. Time for the ancients and for most primitive societies is cyclical and takes its pattern from the succession of day and night and the passing of the

---

[3] Manuel Durán, "El sentido del tiempo en Quevedo," *Cuadernos Americanos,* 63 (1954), 273-88; Charles Marcilly, 71-85; and Kelley, 36-80.

[4] Erwin Panofsky, "Father Time," in *Studies in Iconology* (New York: Harper Torchbook, 1967), 69-94, and G. J. Whitrow, *The Nature of Time* (Harmondsworth, England: Penguin Books, 1975), 11-25.

seasons. It considers time as a creative and productive provider that continually renews and replenishes, creating light from night and the rebirth of life in the spring from the death of winter. This concept dominates the thinking of primitive cultures and produces the allied concepts of the ages of man, ages of history, metempsychosis, and so forth. The concept of cyclical time was incorporated into the church calendar which celebrates the annual birth, death, and resurrection of God.[5]

Opportunity. A third type of time noted by Panofsky is the unstable disordered world of opportunity and chance—the undeserved good and bad fortune that befalls man. This time out of joint was represented in antiquity by the goddess Occasio. Not accidentally did Occasio take on the iconography of the goddess Fortuna until the two merged into one figure.[6] Fortuna was the goddess symbolizing disorder and injustice, and as such came into direct conflict with the Christian concept of a providentially planned world ordered by a supreme being. Fortuna was the only pagan deity to survive into the Christian Middle Ages and Renaissance, undoubtedly because it is so difficult to see a divine plan in the flux of human affairs. Fortune was needed to represent all that was disordered in man's life and was used to explain all the mutable things of the world and man's attachment to them through his passions. This unstable world of opportunity and chance along with the irrational succession of events must be suffered by the

[5] Whitrow, *Natural Philosophy,* 39-41; George Kubler, *The Shape of Time* (New Haven: Yale University Press, 1975); and Mircea Eliade, *The Myth of the Eternal Return, or Cosmos and History* (Princeton: Princeton University Press, 1974).

[6] Panofsky, *Studies,* 69-94, and Rudolf Wittkower, "Chance, Time and Virtue," in *Allegory and the Migration of Symbols* (Boulder: Westview Press, 1977), 97-106.

unenlightened man because of his emotional attachment to the mutable things of the world. Attempting to establish a continuity in his existence and in himself, man is buffeted about in the "temporal" world of accidental causes, poetically represented as passions or storms and shipwrecks.

Eternal Time. The fourth class of time is eternity, the truly timeless world of perfection in which there no longer exists the progression of cause and effect for marking the passage of time, or dividing time into past and future. Nothing begins or ends. According to traditional theology, time was eternal until the Fall.[7] God did not create time, for there is no past, present or future in God's mind where all events are ever present in each moment and eternally. The creation of seasons and adverse climate, and hence of time, occurred at the moment of man's disobedience which introduced death, aging and the seasons into the world. Calderón dramatized repeatedly the creation of time in his *autos sacramentales.* In *El veneno y la triaca,* the four seasons go abreast in eternal harmony until the Fall, when they decide that, because of the changed times, one of them must be on guard while the others rest, even though the flow of time can hardly give them rest.[8] In *El divino Orfeo,* one of the results of the Fall is that the days of creation no longer walk abreast, but decide to proceed in single file, and are transformed into the succession of the days of the week. As they proceed, La Culpa dances between them, her black cape which represents man's sin punctuates the progression of days with the blackness of night. La Naturaleza Humana asks the first day to stop,

[7] Alfred Vacant, *Dictionnaire de théologie catholique* (Paris: Letousey et Ané, 1905).

[8] Calderón de la Barca, *Autos sacramentales,* in *Obras,* III (Madrid: Aguilar, 1967), 191b.

but he is hurried on by night in the figure of La Culpa, which mankind experiences for the first time as "la imagen to mi inobediencia" (1849b). These allegories dramatize the creation of the progression of time, for in eternal time there are not even causes followed by effects or events to mark the passage of time. It is a stable world that is not subject to the progression of cyclical time, rather it is represented as existing eternally as a cycle fixed at full tide and prosperity.

Time becomes a major theme in the pastoral which clearly illustrates the conflict between various temporal concepts. An understanding of the emotional tension in these conflicts provides an excellent background for understanding the anguish that time produces in Baroque poetry. The reexamination of the so-called timelessness of the pastoral in the light of the four concepts of time distinguished previously shows that rather than a simple timeless world removed from daily care, it proves to be a confluence of different kinds of time. Man does not escape from himself and his existence without carrying with him the structures of his known life, whether they continue to exist through negation or through idealization. While the seventeenth-century poet seems to have felt an existential anguish when faced with the destructive forces of a linear irreversible succession of events, the Renaissance poet seems to have been more preoccupied with being held prisoner by his passions to the disordered ebb and flow of irrational events in this world. A study of the temporal determinants in the pastoral poem shows that it does not present a simple timeless world, as is so often repeated, but rather contrasts various types of idealized static time, either cyclical or eternal, with the destructive irrational movement of accidental time. Most often, it presents the idealized cyclical time of the mythical golden age when nature and time were creative, continually returning in sequential regenerative cycles. For this reason, the description of the dawn occurs with such frequency.

Garcilaso's first eclogue presents clearly two different concepts of escapist time.[9] The poem begins at dawn, the time of regeneration:

> Saliendo de las ondas encendido,
> rayaba de los montes el altura
> el sol, cuando Salicio... (43-45)[10]

The sixth stanza describes the natural cyclical time of sunrise and the animals and man returning to their customary activities:

> El sol tiende los rayos de su lumbre
> por montes y por valles, despertando
> las aves y animales y la gente:
> cuál por el aire claro va volando,
> cuál por el verde valle o alta cumbre
> paciendo va segura y libremente,
>   cuál con el sol presente
>   va de nuevo al oficio
>   y al usado ejercicio
> do su natura o menester l'inclina. (71-80)

Salicio presents an idealized vision of the primitive agricultural society freed from anxiety and poverty, in

---

[9] Several studies deal with time in this eclogue. Curiously enough, only one of them touches on the themes treated here. Audrey Lumsden-Kouvel ("Nature and Time in Garcilaso de la Vega," *KRQ*, 19 [1972], 199-209) treats the differences between cyclical and passionate time as a conventional theme in the first part of the eclogue, as well as in other works of Virgil, Sannazzaro, and Garcilaso. The other two studies (Cesare Segre, "Análisis conceptual de la I Egloga de Garcilaso," in *Las estructuras y el tiempo* [Barcelona: Editorial Planeta, 1976], 163-84; and Robert Ter Horst, "Time and Tactics of Supense in Garcilaso's *Egloga primera*," *MLN*, 83 [1968], 145-63) deal with the structure of temporal sequences in the work itself. See also Joseph R. Jones, "'Human Time' in *La Diana*," *RN*, X (1968), 139-46.

[10] All cites come from Garcilaso de la Vega, *Poesías castellanas completas,* ed. Elias L. Rivers (Madrid: Clásicos Castalia, 1969).

which man and animals are integrated into the cycles of natural creative time. As he views these activities, he laments that he cannot be a part of them because his love keeps him subjected to the disordered world of his passions:

> siempre está en llanto esta ánima mezquina,
> cuando la sombra el mundo va cubriendo,
>> o la luz se avecina. (81-3)

No matter what time, day or night, is physically present, the poet cannot be integrated into it, for he is subjected to the *contretemps* of Fortune, by reason of his passionate love. His alienation from nature prevents him from forming a part of the cyclical sequences of time (Kouvel, 157-8).

In the second part of the eclogue, Nemoroso laments the death of his mistress. Through death she has escaped from the temporal world into eternity, and the shepherd, left behind to suffer her loss, wishes to join her and escape from the pain of separation. In contrasting his suffering with the glory that his mistress is enjoying, he laments the fleetingness of the things of the world: "¡Oh bien caduco, vano y presuroso!"(256). He continually recalls the night of her death which torments him, but since he is tied to the insecurities of life, he imagines her observing the fluctuations of the earth from the immovable Heavens:

> Divina Elisa, pues agora el cielo
> con inmortales pies pisas y mides,
> y su mudanza ves, estando queda.... (394-6)

He wonders why she does not speed up time so he will die and join her, and together in the heaven of lovers (the sphere of Venus) they will seek solace in another better pastoral world, freed from the uncertainties of earthly existence:

116

¿Por qué de mí te olvidas y no pides
que se apresure el tiempo en que este velo
rompa del cuerpo y verme libre pueda,
　　　y en la tercera rueda,
　　　contigo mano a mano,
busquemos otros montes y otros ríos,
otros valles floridos y sombríos
donde descanse y siempre pueda verte.　(397-405)

Garcilaso's two shepherds have traditionally been interpreted as a splitting of his psyche into the two types of grief he experienced, first on being rejected by Isabel Freire when she married, and second on the occasion of her death.[11] The analysis of the time determinants in the eclogue show that the poet conceived of each psychological state as an alienation from an idealized time, either the bountiful cycles of nature or the unchanging immobility of eternity. In each case, the poet is subjected to the misfortune and grief of the instability of the temporal world. Unlike the seventeenth-century poet, he is not tormented by the the brevity of life or the destruction implied by a linear time. Rather it is the disordered world of accidents and misfortune from which he cannot escape, either to reintegrate himself into the cycles of nature or to enjoy the stability of eternal life.

The same duality of idealized time is present in the poetry of Fray Luis de León. In his *Vida retirada* he struggles to free himself from the disordered temporal world and live peacefully in the natural world of cyclical time. He seeks the world of natural uninterrupted sleep: "Un no rompido sueño, / un día puro, alegre, libre quiero..." (26-7).[12] And he wishes to commit himself to

---

[11]　Rafael Lapesa, *La trayectoria poética de Garcilaso* (Madrid: Revista de Occidente, 1968), 130.

[12]　All cites come from Fray Luis de León, *Poesías,* ed. Angel Custodio Vega (Madrid: Cupsa Editorial, 1976).

the natural rhythms of country life, and free himself from the cares of the world:

> Despiértenme las aves
> con su cantar süave no aprendido;
> no los cuidados graves
> de que es siempre seguido
> quien al ajeno arbitrio está atenido. (31-5)

In this way he can live freed from his passions:

> Vivir quiero conmigo,
> gozar quiero del bien que debo al cielo,
> a solas, sin testigo,
> libre de amor, de celo,
> de odio, de esperanzas, de recelo. (36-41)

He devotes five stanzas to the description of the garden at La Flecha, presented as a pastoral paradise, in spring time at full bloom. All the elements of nature contribute to its fullness: the fountain waters it and the breezes carry its scents to the poet. The title of the poem and the description of the garden are often taken to be the substance of the poem, but such a reading overlooks the fact that nearly half the poem describes the urbane world of passion from which he wants to escape, and which he characterizes as "aqueste mar tempestuoso" (25). In line 21, he evokes the beauty of nature and each of the following four stanzas are divided into two parts, in the first half of each he presents the glory of nature, but the second half condemns the slavery to life's commitments. Immediately following the description of the garden are two stanzas describing a storm at sea which man suffers to satisfy his greed. Paradoxically, the storm is evoked precisely at the moment in which the vision of the garden has lulled him into forgetting the strife caused by the desire for wealth and power: "un manso rüido / que del oro y del cetro pone olvido" (58-9). The very act of forgetting, the word "olvido" itself, serves only to remind him in full detail of the storms that he must endure in this life, and the following two stanzas describe the horrors of a sea-storm.

Even more equivocal is the succession of imperative verbs, especially in the final pastoral vision in which he describes his felicity: "Despiértenme las aves" (31), "una pobre mesa...me baste" (71-3), and "tendido yo a la sombra esté cantando" (80). These commands place the garden and retirement on the level of wished for, but unattained, escapist fantasies. The poet does praise the simple country life and he condemns the conflicts and confusion of urban life, but he realizes, on an unstated level, that he is committed to his urban existence. The poem sets up a tension between the irrational flux of events in a life committed to gain and achievement, and the commonsense rejection of that world in favor of a pastoral world based on natural cycles. The tension is not resolved as the verb tenses place the pastoral paradise in the realm of unachieved fantasy. The *Vida retirada* is not an ecstatic espousal of the perfect world of nature, rather it represents the struggle, probably unsuccessful, to escape from the destructive disordered world of commitment into the creative cyclical world.

Like the *Vida retirada* which contrasts two concepts of time, one irrational and the other cyclical, so does the Tenth Ode dedicated to Felipe Ruiz describe the eternal motionless firmament and contrast it with the storms and violence of the earth. He states first that he wishes to escape from life: "¿Cuándo será que pueda / libre de esta prisión volar al cielo...?" (1-2), and also from the succession of events: "veré distinto y junto / lo que es y lo que ha sido, / y su principio propio y ascondido" (8-10). From Heaven he will be able to observe the disruptions— earthquakes, storms and tides—of the physical world:

> Por qué tiembla la tierra,
> por qué las hondas mares se embravecen,
> do sale a mover guerra
> el cierzo, y por qué crecen
> las aguas del océano y descrecen. (21-5)

But he will be in a world in which movement, and hence time, do not exist: "Veré, sin movimiento / la más alta esfera, las moradas / del gozo y del contento" (66-8). In the Eighteenth Ode, *Morada del cielo,* he longs again to join the world of eternal time presented as a timeless pastoral world, freed from the temporal inconveniences of the physical world:

> Alma región luciente,
> prado de bienandanza, que ni al hielo
> ni con el rayo ardiente
> fallece.... (1-4)

It is a perfect world, ever reproducing itself and freed from the succession of cause and effect that mark time for the temporal world:

> El va, en pos dichosas
> le siguen sus ovejas, do las pace
> con inmortales rosas,
> con flor que siempre nace,
> y cuanto más se goza más renace. (11-5)

Fray Luis admirably characterizes the various types of time, from the passionate world full of seasonal changes and accidental storms, to the natural cycles of nature and the static unchanging life of eternity. Like Garcilaso, he presents himself as trapped by worldly temporal passions, and his odes show a longing to escape from the irrational but dominating forces of the temporal world into the cyclical time of the pastoral or the static time of the eternalized pastoral.

Lope de Vega's *Egloga Segunda,* published in his

Rimas (1602), shows the same desire to escape from worldly time as do Garcilaso and Fray Luis de León, but, in addition to developing the destruction and instability of the shepherd's emotional attachment to his passions, Lope adds a new note of the brevity of life. Not only does the poet suffer from not being a part of the natural regenerative cycles, but he is also a hostage of a fleeting time that will eventually destroy his life. Lope introduces this typical Baroque theme in spite of the fact that his eclogue is an extended gloss on the sixth stanza of Garcilaso's *Egloga I*. In this stanza, previously cited, Salicio observes the beginning of the day, the start of cyclical time, and laments that he cannot find a place in the world, be it day or night. Lope amplifies this idea by dedicating the whole eclogue to the description of the different times of the day, and giving reasons why the poet cannot find comfort in the solitude of primitive cyclical time, and actually suffers from the thought of a time that will destroy him.

Elisio begins offering himself as a sacrifice to his beloved, but disdainful, Lucinda. As he weeps over his pitiful desperation, the sun begins to rise and he greets the dawn by praising the light. He had hoped that the light would dispel the sadness he had suffered during the night, but "mi dolor renuevo / viendo que sale el día / y que comienzo a padecer de nuevo" (28-30).[13] After describing his misery and suffering, he dedicates each of three stanzas to different times of the day: dawn, midday, and night. Each stanza contains a description of the typical activities of that time of day and at the end of each he laments that he can find no part in these activities. He describes the harmony of the birds and animals, and the peace of the world at dawn, but concludes:

---

[13] Lope de Vega, *Obras poéticas,* 173-6.

Yo, triste, en este suelo
tendido, sin saber si parte o sale,
de todo bien me privo;
ninguna luz me vale;
siempre en tinieblas y en tormento vivo. (56-60)

In the next stanza he describes how when Apollo is at the zenith, the animals rest and the activities of the morning fall into a lethargic slumber, but the poor shepherd will not find rest at this hour either:

yo solo entonces, de mi error vencido,
viviré sin descanso,
llorando celos y temiendo olvido. (73-5)

Finally night brings complete calm, the animals sleep peacefully and the laborers return to their cabins, but the lover will continue to suffer:

y veráse, colgada de su filo,
callar la noche helada,
y que no muda mi dolor estilo. (88-90)

The cycles of the day have been described with loving attention to detail, and in each case the poet laments that he does not find peace during any of them. In the next to last stanza, the miserable shepherd, rejected from the natural cycles of time, concludes eloquently that he cannot find a moment's solace from the pains of his love:

"No hay tiempo para mí, faltóme el tiempo;
ya son del mar las olas mis cuidados,
la que se acaba crece en la que viene;
mi frágil esperanza llega a tiempo,
que con pasos enfermos y cansados
huyendo de la muerte se entretiene;
mas poca resistencia le conviene,
que al fin la alcanzará con la sospecha,
y a sus manos deshecha,
quien puede asegurar mi corta vida. (91-100)

In spite of the close relationship of the structure of this eclogue to the previously cited stanza in Garcilaso's *Egloga I,* the conception of time has been slightly modified. Unlike Salicio, Elisio does not recall a former idyllic state when he and Lucinda enjoyed a beautiful relationship. Instead, Lucinda has always abhorred him and refused him her favors. The contrast in this poem is not between a past glory and a present misery, but directly between the harmonious world of cyclical nature and the poet who suffers, unconsoled by the cycles of nature.

Also, Lope's Elisio does not describe his love in terms of uncontrollable passions and violent storms, rather his passion has sapped his strength and he lives in a depressed state whose chief metaphors are dying, weakness and darkness. He is "desnuda de mi propia resistencià' (8), "siempre en tinieblas y en tormentò' (60), and "llorando celos y temiendo olvidò' (75). A bit of hope comes to keep him from death: "mi frágil esperanza llega a tiempo, / que con pasos enfermos y cansados / huyendo de la muerte se entretienè' (94-6). The emphasis has subtly shifted from the tormented irrational time that Garcilaso and Fray Luis characterized as dominating passions and storms at sea to the more typical seventeenth-century concern with a linear destructive time. Lope introduces the concept of the brevity of life when the shepherd exclaims that his lady is the person "quien puede asegurar mi corta vidà' (100), and cries out to her: "Dulcísima homicidà' (101). His love itself is the destructive force that assures his mortality. But, paradoxically, it is also that which sustains his miserable existence. Rather than wishing to forget the lady and integrate himself into the natural cycles of time, he begs her not to destroy any possibility of hope while he lives, because that at least keeps him alive:

> no mates con desdenes mi esperanza,
> antes la vida muera;
> que el bien que no se alcanza,
> al fin es bien, mientras goza se espera. (102-5)

This again reminds us of death and "la corta vida." Lope, amplifying Garcilaso's stanza, has shifted from a desire to escape the irrational time of uncontrollable passion to a preoccupation with the linear time that produces death, decay and sickness. In effect, the sixteenth-century theme of escaping the incessant flow of time through an escape to a primitive idealistic time or an idealized mystical eternity has been supplanted by the seventeenth-century theme of the brevity of life. Lope has upon reworking a pastoral motif expanded the concepts of time so that the pastoral can be said to include all four conceptions of time prevalent in Golden Age poetry.

The employment of time in the pastoral provides an excellent background for understanding the typical Baroque reaction to the insubstantiality of the things of this world. The sixteenth-century poet dreams of a perfection of his existence by rising above his passions and thus escaping the destructive flux of events. Garcilaso sees it in a former love celebrated away from the torments of irrational events or in a future eternity. Fray Luis seeks it in the idyllic country life, be it temporal or eternal. In both cases, the poet is seeking to escape the torments of an uncertain worldly existence. Both poets clearly lament their commitment to worldly things, even though one suspects that Garcilaso tends to ennoble his suffering while Fray Luis spurns the desire for wealth and power in spite of his unfailing commitment to it. The forcefully expressed lack of confidence in the disordered sequence of worldly events and the desire for a new time sequence that would give rest to the soul clearly is a step towards the Baroque disillusionment in the face of a non-transcendent world of flux and change where everything is destroyed by a fleeting incomprehensible flow of time.

All of the Renaissance and Baroque conflicts of time can be viewed as manifestations of the basic dichotomy of the mental conception of static time as opposed to the experience of a fluid ever-moving time. The Renaissance poets contrasted the irrational flow of events with two concepts of static time, either the peaceful cycles of regenerative nature or the complete rest of eternity. The Baroque poet still focuses on the instability of the world about him, but in the field of time, places ever more emphasis on the speed of time and how it destroys worldly existence. The brevity of life tends to be as much a preoccupation as the uncertainties of the passions, and the pastoral evocation of natural cycles tends to be replaced by a desire for the stability and "reality" of eternity. This is clearly the main difference between the "desengañò" of Fray Luis and that of Quevedo. Fray Luis does not show concern for the brevity of life, but longs to escape from life and its tormenting adversities, whereas Quevedo is torn between the conflicting emotions produced by the lack of stability of earthly existence and the fact that this existence is all that can be known by sense experience. Both poets wish to escape the irrationality of the world, but Fray Luis views it as a result of the emotional struggle with the unreality of the world, while Quevedo adds to the idea of a disordered flow of temporal events, the vision of time as a leveler and destroyer of everything that is knowable in this world dominated by man and his works. Both poets show their disillusionment with the world, but each one focuses his preoccupation differently. The conflict between the attractions of the world and the logical choice of retirement is subtly presented by implication in Fray Luis, whereas Quevedo expresses frankly both his desire to aggrandize and perpetuate his life and his amazement and incomprehensibility of why it must perish.

The pastoral poet's encounter with time is neither abstract nor superficial as he attempts to escape the chronology of everyday existence in a new perfected world. The pastoral represents a profound and deeply-felt existential reaction to the confrontation with time—no less so than the Baroque poet's metaphysical anquish in the face of a linear destructive time. The pastoral does not represent a simple flight into a timeless world, but rather it proves to be a confluence of man's conceptions of time elaborated over the tension inherent in the conflict between the destructive nerve-racking time of disordered fortune and chance and the return to the primitive regenerative concept of cyclical time or the redemptive timelessness of eternity.

8. The Sundial and the Hourglass

The task of locating poems whose central image is the clock is facilitated by two anthologies of this image in Spanish poetry. The first is a general anthology by Santos Torroella[1] covering from the Middle Ages to the present day. His conclusion that the clock is not extremely frequent as an image in poetry is somewhat invalidated by the second study by Herrero García[2] which limits its focus to the seventeenth century. He collects and comments on a dozen poems and makes reference to an equal number that he had published previously or planned to publish in the future. Both anthologizers agree that this image has special characteristics in the seventeenth century. Santos Torroella divides the poetry he collects into three periods, and characterizes the first period, the baroque, as emphasizing the ascetic and stoic themes of the brevity of life (XVII).

Two figures stand out in the seventeenth century for their treatment of the theme of the clock. Not surprisingly, Quevedo was one of the ones to treat quite frequently the image of the clock. Many writers dealt with the theme of the brevity of life, but Quevedo is the writer who seems to have felt most deeply the shortness

---

[1] Rafael Santos Torroella, ed., *Los números del tiempo. Antología del reloj y las horas en la poesía castellana* (Madrid: Roberto Carbonell Blasco, 1953).

[2] Miguel Herrero García, *El reloj en la vida española* (Madrid: Roberto Carbonell Blasco, 1955).

and futility of human existence, and to have treated the problem with the most poignancy.[3] His three *silvas,* "El reloj de arena," "Reloj de campanilla," and "El reloj de sol," treat the three types of clocks common in his time, and provide a kind of history of the development of the clock from the sundial to the mechanical clock. In all three poems, the final conceits are of a depth and style worthy of his best metaphysical sonnets.

The other figure, Francisco de la Torre y Sevil, is a minor Valencian poet.[4] Born before 1620 in Tortosa, he lived in Valencia where he was a counselor and favorite of the viceroy, and he was knighted as a member of the Order of Calatrava. He resided in Madrid from 1674 and died before 1682. He published several volumes of poetry and wrote several *comedias,* but he is most famous for his two volumes of translations of the Latin epigrams of John Owen, to which he often added one or more epigrams of his own invention. His development as a translator of epigrams gave his own poetry a certain terseness of expression that at times approaches the metaphysical mode. The reason for his fascination with timepieces is not easily extracted from his poetry. Some of his early poems are based on rather humble imagery, such as the sonnets dealing with dice, swords, and firearms, but this does not explain his interest in clocks.[5]

Unlike Quevedo, he does not seem to have had a great personal preoccupation with time. He did write an

---

[3] Manuel Durán, "El sentido del tiempo en Quevedo," *Cuadernos Americanos,* 73 (1954), 273-88.

[4] The biographical facts are taken from Cayetano Alberto de la Barrera y Leirado, *Catálogo bibliográfico y biográfico del teatro antiguo español* (Madrid, 1860; fsml. rpt.: Madrid: Gredos, 1969), 399-402 and *Enciclopedia Espasa.*

[5] Feniso de la Torre [Francisco de la Torre y Sevil], ed., *Entretenimiento de las musas en esta baraxa nueva de versos* (Zaragoza: Juan de Ybar, 1654), 5, 51, and 53.

occasional poem on ruins, but it seems to have been more an exercise in "desengaño" than a deeply felt piece. He translated two epigrams of Owen on time, and added to each of them an epigram of his own on the same theme, but their abstract style does not reveal a personal concern.

One of Torre y Sevil's additions to an epigram by Owen on the brevity of life reveals his own poetic style:

ADD. A LA BREVEDAD DE LA VIDA

Es la vida impresión, cuya escritura
humo, y puntos señala en su argumento,
música de Eco su partida aliento,
mármol de espuma es su arquitectura.

Pronto celaje, que una aurora dura,
delgado vidro, que fabrica el viento,
leve barro, si voy al fundamento,
rápida flor, si miro la hermosura.

Veloz nube rompida en vanos truenos,
vaga sombra del sol apresurada,
que cuando es más, es menos que lo menos,
y cuando es algo, es todo lo que es nada.[6]

In the poem, he compiles a series of images to which he compares the substance of life, such as writing in smoke, an echo of music, a statue of foam, and delicate glass made in the wind. Its basis is insubstantial clay, its beauty a passing flower. Some of the images are startling in their juxtaposition of elements, such as "rápida flor," and "mármol de espuma." Others are poetically quite beautiful, while others suggest other contexts, such as the "vaga sombra," which recalls the Platonic myths of the world and life as a shadowy existence. The imagery is summarized or concluded by a couplet of abstract *conceptista* reasoning typical of Owen's epigrammatic

---

6 Juan Oven, *Agudezas,* trans. Francisco de la Torre [y Sevil] (Madrid: Francisco Sanz, 1674), 366-7.

style. The poem is interesting for a discussion of Torre y Sevil's attitude towards clocks because it shows him expanding his thought in his own poetic style. While the images are admirable, they do not convey the same feeling of anguish as those of Quevedo. In fact, they give the impression of being carefully thought out and composed, whereas Quevedo's imagery of the brevity of life strikes the reader as a personal, deeply felt response. In spite of his rather academic sensitivity to time and the brevity of life, his numerous poems on clocks reveal a real fascination with the symbol of the passage of time.

The study of the imagery of primitive clocks in seventeenth-century poetry shows two stylistic tendencies at the beginning of the seventeenth century: one strongly moral in tone uses the image to reiterate traditional religious morality, while the other is metaphysical poetry which, while still didactic, is more philosophical and tends to emphasize man's existential anguish and the paradoxical nature of time. The metaphysical mode has a definite relationship to the traditional moral poetry which, following the norms of Counterreformation aesthetics, tried to make its message more relevant and real through the use of concrete imagery. Once poets such as Quevedo and Góngora freed this imagery from its moral implications to make points about man's secular position in the world, a true metaphysical style of poetry came into existence. During the course of the century, this poetry lost its philosophical base and evolved into an extravagant type of *conceptismo* relying on far-fetched comparisons that were barren of significant ideas, and as such signaled the demise of metaphysical poetry in Spain.

The Sundial

Sun clocks were used extensively in the ancient world and their popularity in the Renaissance and later is attested by the appearance of over half a dozen Spanish treatises in the sixteenth, seventeenth, and early eighteenth centuries explaining their construction and use; in fact, the first treatise in Spanish on the mechanical clock appeared as late as 1759.[7] Even though mechanical clocks were installed on Spanish cathedral towers from the late fourteenth century onwards, they were not at all reliable for short intervals of time, and for that reason, the sundial and hourglass continued to be used extensively (Crombie, 1959: II, 98). In spite of its simple appearance, the sundial was very sophisticated and quite accurate. Cristóbal Suárez de Figueroa gave an idea of the complexity of calculations necessary for its construction:

> Mas para entender de relojes, conviene tener noticia de los ángulos horarios, de los arcos horizontales (que los Arabes llaman Azimut), de los verticales, del diurno, de la ascensión recta, de la oblicua, de las declinaciones, y distancias de longitud y latitud del sol; de los días naturales y artificiales, … de las distancias, de las horas, de los grados, de las horas equinociales, antemeridianas, postmeridianas, ineguales, occidentales; del horóscopo, del nemón, o estilo, de la mira de las líneas rectas y perpendiculares, de la línea del horizonte, de la meridiana, de la del estilo, o mira del nadir, que es el punto opuesto a la eclíptica del zenit, o vertex, que es el punto en el cielo derechamente a nuestra cabeza; del

---

[7] Luis Montañez Fontenla, *Museo español de antigüedades* (Madrid: s.i., 1964), 18.

seno recto, oblicuo y reverso; de la superficie meridional, de
la sombra versa y recta; de cosas tales necesarias en materia
de relojes.[8]

Tomás Vicente Tosca, seventeenth-century mathematician, paraphrases a passage from antiquity that shows
the sophistication of the readings:

> ...dando de esta suerte a conocer en cualquier clima varios
> géneros de horas; el aumento y disminución de los días; el
> signo y punto que en su eclíptica tiene el sol; el vertical y
> paralelo en que se halla a cualquier hora; la casa del cielo que
> ocupa; el signo que asciende por el oriente o desciende por el
> ocaso, y otras maravillas semejantes que se verán en este
> tratado. (Montañez, 1964: 6)

None of the poems on the sundial employs such specific
readings; rather they simply moralize the image of the
light falling on the pointer, variously called "índice,"
"nemón," or "estilo de mira."

Covarrubias' Emblema 74 from Book III shows a
sundial in a desolate area with the sun shining on it,
bearing the motto "Dum lucet," as long as it shines. He
moralizes the sun as justice and life:

> El reloj que es de sol, poco aprovecha
> en cuanto de sus rayos no le envía
> su luz, que en el nemón, dando derecha,
> señalara las horas por el día;
> y así en aquesta vida, el que deshecha
> la santa inspiración, y no se guía
> por el sol verdadero de justicia,
> dejarle ha a la sombra su malicia.
>
> (Covarrubias, 1610: 274)

In the prose commentary, Covarrubias reveals that the

---

8 Christóbal Suárez de Figueroa, trans. *Plaza universal de todas ciencias
y artes* (Perpiñan: Luys Rouve, 1629), 330v. The title says it was "parte
traduzida de Toscano y parte compuesta." The original is by Tomasso
Garzoni.

motto comes from John 12:35-6: "Walk whilst you have the light, that the darkness overtake you not. And he that walketh in darkness knoweth not whither he goeth. Whilst you have the light, believe in the light, that you may be children of the light." He interprets the emblem with its poem as a kind of spiritual "carpe diem." Man must work while the sun of justice is shining. The wit of the emblem consists of the attribution of a double meaning to the sun. It is both life: "...la luz, que es el curso de esta vida," and it is divine illumination from God: "Aquel sol de justicia, que nos envía sus rayos de claridad, y calor divino, con santas y buenas inspiraciones" (274v). Thus, man must take advantage of the light, which is both his life and spiritual guide; otherwise he will be dead, both physically and spiritually: "si sobrevienen las tinieblas de la noche, que es la muerte, no será ya tiempo de obrar, ni de merecer." The relative simplicity of the ideas presented achieves poetic depth in the double meaning given to the light.

Francisco de la Torre y Sevil added two short poems to his translation of the epigram in which Owen allegorized solar and lunar eclipses as a lapse into the shadow of sin. Torre's second addition further compounds the conceit by including the element of time. In it he moralizes an eclipse of the light on a sundial by a passing cloud:

OTRA A UN RELOJ DE SOL

La nube que al Sol se opone
en el Reloj obscurece
las horas; éste parece
símbolo que te propone:
que si el vicio se antepone
por ti a la virtud, desdoras
el bien que en ella atesoras,
pues vil nube tu malicia
se opone al Sol de Justicia,
y te hace perder las horas. (Oven, 1682: 119)

133

He sees the cloud as an image of sin obscuring the light of virtue, "vil nube tu malicia," and the shadow cast down by evil as preventing us from enjoying God's grace. The repetition of the verb "oponerse" emphasizes the dual function of the verb as a reference to the shadow, the cloud's moving in front of the sun and to sin, the opposite or contrary of the light of justice. Likewise, the repetition of "las horas" suggests a multiple meaning—first of the darkness preventing one from reading the hours on the sundial and secondly the loss of one's life by squandering it. Also implicit is the idea of not praying the canonical hours because sin and loss of grace prevent one from enjoying communion with God. Like Covarrubias' emblem, Torre's *décima* moralizes the shadow as evil and the loss of light as the loss of grace which makes it impossible for man to enjoy his life to the fullest extent.

Attributed to Góngora is a *décima* to the "reloj de sol," included among the descriptions of the various types of clocks. Less moralizing and more metaphysical, the poet stresses not the spiritual life, but the paradox of the passage of time and the shortness of life:

DE SOL

¡Con qué mano liberal,
si bien de hierro pesado,
las horas que nos has dado
contando vas puntual!
El camino puntual
del desengaño más fuerte
señalas; y porque acierte
la vida ciega que pasa,
con sol le muestras su casa
por las sombras de la muerte.[9]

---

[9]   Góngora, 1961: 434. Line 5 is one syllable short.

134

He addresses the pointer of the timepiece, calling it a generous hand freely dispensing hours, but at the same time, he recalls that it is made of heavy iron and counts precisely the passing hours. The contrast between "liberal" and "pesado" represents man's inner psychological reaction to the flow of time. On the one hand it seems there is sufficient time, even on occasion too much, thus, the hours are freely dispensed; but on reflection, every passing moment is a loss that causes grief and sadness. This psychological conflict prepares for the deeper paradox, the lesson of "desengaño" that one should see in the image of the clock. The sundial marks with precision the path of the sun, "el camino puntual," which is also the path of life, this path cannot be seen until illuminated by the sun and read on the clock. The poet notes that the sundial not only tells the time of day but it also reveals the position or house of the sun in the zodiac, thus recalling that the sun also measures the seasons and the ages of man. As the pointer marks the progression of the sun, it does so with the very symbol of death, the shadow.

Rather than moralize the image of the sundial, the poet sees in it a metaphysical image that reminds us of impending death, not only in the fact that it counts out the hours of life, but also in the symbolic aspects of the apparatus. Thus, he combines mechanical function and contrived symbol to point to the same meaning.

Quevedo's *silva* on the sun clock displays even more fully the metaphysical style, and is undoubtedly one of the best poems on clocks:

EL RELOJ DE SOL

¿Ves, Floro, que, prestando Arismética
números a la docta Geometría,
los pasos de la luz le cuenta al día?

135

¿Ves por aquella línea, bien fijada
a su meridiano y a su altura,   5
del sol al velocísima hermosura
con certeza espiada?
¿Agradeces curioso
el saber cuánto vives,
y la luz y las horas recibes?   10
Empero si olvidares, estudioso,
con pensamiento ocioso,
el saber cuánto mueres,
ingrato a tu vivir y morir eres:
pues tu vida, si atiendes su doctrina,   15
camina al paso que su luz camina.
No cuentes por sus líneas solamente
las horas, sino lógrelas tu mente;
pues en él, recordada,
ves tu muerte en tu vida retratada,   20
cuando tú, que eres sombra,
pues la santa Verdad ansí te nombra,
como la sombra suya, peregrino,
desde un número en otro tu camino
corres, y pasajero,   25
te aguarda sombra el número postrero. (122-3)

The poem is addressed to a rhetorical Floro whose name
suggests all the poetical flowers that, by living for one
day only, become symbols of transience. The first seven
lines describe the clock and its measurement of the
movement of the sun. The sciences of arithmetic and
geometry, two of the four liberal arts of the medieval
quadrivium, combine to make possible the reading. The
word "altura" (5) has two possible interpretations. First
it may indicate a cylindrical sun clock. There were two
kinds of sun clocks, the flat type with a vertical pointer
most commonly seen today and a cylindrical type with a
horizontal pointer. In this reading, "altura" would refer
to the height of the shadow on the cylinder. The more
likely interpretation would be that the phrases "a su
meridiano" and "a su altura" equivocally refer to both

the "línea," the shadow on the clock, and to the sun itself which is at full ascent at midday, suggesting the fullness of life, and a forthcoming descent and decline. Even at the period of life in full bloom, one must look to the constant movement of time and encroaching decay. Even though the line on the clock is "bien fijada," at the same time it shows the speed of the sun, thus embodying the dichotomy of the immobile and the transient. The sun seems not to move, and the pointer fixedly determines its position, but at the same time records its movement. The one, the fixed moment, actually turns into a progression of many moments. The word "espiada" plays on the word "espía," the drum wheel of the mechanical weight-driven clock that brings in and lets out the cord. Here the phrase "espiada con certeza" refers both to the reader as an observer who secretly spies on the sun in order to observe the exactness of its movement, and to the movement itself which is controlled, "espiada con certeza." The comparison makes of the sun a huge clock by attributing to it the "espía," one of the regulatory devices of a mechanical clock.

Lines 8 through 16 introduce the conceit of life as a process of dying. The clock measures out the light and hours of Floro's life, thus satisfying his curiosity, but as a student of life he should not forget that the clock also measures his death because each hour is a dying, a step towards the end of the light. The next four lines (17-20) advise the transient reader not just to count the hours, but to "lograrlas," that is, to take advantage of them, by realizing their importance. He then returns to the concept that life is actually a process of dying, and this is seen in the sun clock very clearly once one has its image in his mind. Line 21 introduces the word "sombra" which he has carefully withheld until this point. All previous references to the sun dial have been to the pointer or to the light. Now Quevedo urges the reader to ponder the image of the shadow on the clock. The Holy Scriptures call man a shadow, and man like the shadow on the sun clock will run from one number to the other, passing each by until the last number when all falls into shadow. As there are two shadows on the sun dial, the one during the day that measures time, and the other at nightfall that obliterates time, so too does man have two shadowy existences. His body is a shadow, a reflection of light, and upon his death he passes into the land of shadows. The day measured out by the sun clock is the brief day of man's existence, and the clock is emblematic of that existence. Time is measured and speeds quickly during the light, but at the end all falls into darkness and timelessness. Man must note with anxiety the passage of each hour, for time weighs on his memory as an image of death when he passes into eternity and time itself ceases to exist.

This is one of Quevedo's finest metaphysical poems. The dichotomy of the one and the many is clearly portrayed in the double significance given to the concept of the shadow. He skillfully witholds the introduction of the word ''sombra'' until near the end of the poem and does not introduce its second meaning of death until the very last word where it comes as a shock as the reader realizes the full implications of the imagery, much the same way that he will be surprised by his own death. The self-assured reader is asked to reenact his life in the process of the poem, realizing indeed that time flees and he must take advantage of its moments. In essence, he knew this from the beginning, but the surprise of the end, the revelation of the final shadow obliterating time and life, is meant to shake the reader's self-confidence with the revelation that in spite of his acceptance of the message on an intellectual plane, he was still unprepared for the final emotional twist. The essence of "desengaño" is the realization of the insubstantiality of life, and Quevedo produces in the process of reading the poem the very emotional response that he has been conveying as an intellectual message.

The image of the sundial evokes more or less the same poetical allegories, but the overall effect is different. Covarrubias and Torre y Sevil extracted a spiritual message "a lo divino," seeing the sunlight as grace and the shadow as sin, whereas Góngora and Quevedo presented the metaphysical paradox of the one and the many as manifested in the psychological perception of time. They both present the sun as a giver and counter of life and the shadows as constant reminders that the sum total of the reckoning is the end of one's personal existence. Góngora, however, focuses on the paradox of the perception of the instant contrasted with the constant movement of time, whereas Quevedo emphasizes the personal response to the passage of time. For all the poets, the sundial not only shows the advance of life, but also serves as a warning: either an admonishment to avoid sin, or a reminder of one's final destruction.

The Hourglass

The hourglass, even less so than the sundial, may not seem to pertain to a study of mechanical imagery in poetry. Neither does it require the fine calibrations of the sundial nor is it a machine utilizing mechanical parts. Its importance, however, as a part of the theme of the clock cannot be overlooked. The hourglass is the only marker which visually shows the passage of time, thus, it imparts a special anxiety as time silently slipping from its container is actually observed.

The hourglass is in reality a later invention than the mechanical clock, but its relatively simplified nature places it before the true mechanical clock:

> Sandglasses first appeared in the fourteenth century and are still broadly used. In the earliest example, two separate glass bulbs were bound together at their necks, having a metal plate with a pierced hole clamped in between. One may look at such a device as the combination of an outflow and inflow clepsydra, with fine sand replacing water or mercury. (Fraser, 1975: 55)

Generally, the image of the clock enters into seventeenth-century poetry because of the preoccupation with time rather than an interest in mechanics. Even so, some aspect of the timepiece occasionally provides a precise analogy to an idea, as in this image by Bocángel:

> Sale el fuego del pecho, y vuelve al pecho,
> cual reloj, que hilando las arenas,
> las mismas otra vez en si recibe.

Porque faltaran al amor sospecho,
ya penas contra mí, y así apercibe,
que en mí como en reloj vivan las penas.[10]

He uses the image of an hourglass to describe how his amorous passion can leave his heart, be replaced by tears, but later return to torment him, that is, how fire can turn to water, and back to fire. Showing little interest in the passage of time, he uses the sand in the hourglass as a visual representation of his emotional changes, creating a purely mechanical image of an analogous physical process.

The *décima* attributed to Góngora on the "reloj de arena" initiates the series entitled "Medida del tiempo por diferentes relojes." In this brief poem, the poet summarizes admirably the paradox of the mind's ability to conceptualize fixed time, which in turn recalls the contrasting image of the inevitable flow of time:

RELOJ DE ARENA

¿Qué importa, oh Tiempo tirano,
aquel calabozo estrecho
que de vidrio te hemos hecho
para tenerte en la mano,
si el detenerte es en vano
y siempre de ti está ajena,
cuando más piensa que llena
nuestra vida, a cuya voz
huyes cual tiempo veloz,
y sordo, como en arena? (Góngora, 1961: 433-4)

The poem is addressed not to the timepiece, but to time itself which the poet envisions as a tyrant dominating life.

---

[10] Bocángel, vol. 1, 260. He used the same expression "hilando arena" in another poem: "ejemplar / de reloj, que hilando arenas, / es su fin su comenzar." (316)

141

The hourglass is a confining jail for the purpose of containing time and holding it in our hands. But such an effort is useless since time cannot be stopped. The more the hourglass fills, the more time that accumulates, the less of life that remains. The poet cries out in anguish as time steals away silently on sand. This poem deals marvelously with the paradox of the movement of time and man's attempts to create static time. The image gives visual form to both concepts, and shows the impossibility of stopping fleeting time.

One of the epigrams of John Owen translated by Torre y Sevil draws a psychological point about time:

RELOJ DE ARENA

El cierto Reloj de arena,
miente, porque el agujero,
con el tiempo siempre es más,
y siempre la arena es menos. (Oven, 1674: 253)

Even though the "clepsydra" is very exact, "cierto," in fact, it deceives us because with time, as the sand grows less, it seems that the opening grows larger. The paradox comes from the observation that at first the sand seems to fall very slowly and the quantity above decreases very little, but when the upper bulb is nearly empty, the sand seems to flow more rapidly. He conceptualizes the apparent increase in speed by claiming that the size of the hole increases as the amount of sand diminishes. This represents in visual imagery the psychological fact that at the beginning of a time period, it seems that there is always sufficient time, but towards the end, one sees there is little time remaining and its speed seems to increase.

Quevedo's *silva* "El reloj de arena" exists in two versions, the earlier one dating from before 1611.[11] The two versions are evidence that Quevedo was interested enough in the piece to rework it, and it is probable that this was the first of the three *silvas* and that he later added the companion pieces of the sandglass and mechanical clock. The later version is shorter and more concise in expression:

EL RELOJ DE ARENA

¿Qué tienes que contar, reloj molesto,
en un soplo de vida desdichada
que se pasa tan presto;
en un camino que es una jornada,
breve y estrecha, de este al otro polo,   5
siendo jornada que es un paso solo?
Que, si son mis trabajos y mis penas,
no alcanzarás allá, si capaz vaso
fueses de las arenas
en donde el alto mar detiene el paso.   10
Deja pasar las horas sin sentirlas,
que no quiero medirlas,
ni que me notifiques de esa suerte
los términos forzosos de la muerte.
No me hagas más guerra;   15
déjame, y nombre de piadoso cobra,
que harto tiempo me sobra
para dormir debajo de la tierra.
Pero si por acaso por oficio tienes
el contarme la vida,   20
presto descansarás, que los cuidados
mal acondicionados,
que alimenta lloroso
el corazón cuitado y lastimoso,
y la llama atrevida   25

[11] Francisco de Quevedo, *Obra poética,* I, ed. José Manuel Blecua (Madrid: Editorial Castalia, 1969), 270.

que Amor, ¡triste de mí!, arde en mis venas
(menos de sangre que de fuego llenas),
no sólo me apresura
la muerte, pero abréviame el camino;
pues, con pie doloroso,   30
mísero peregrino,
doy cercos a la negra sepultura.
Bien sé que soy aliento fugitivo;
ya sé, ya temo, ya también espero
que he de ser polvo, como tú, si muero,   35
y que soy vidro, como tú, si vivo. (119-20)

The revised text is less intensely personal, substituting "la muerte" (l4) for "mi muerte," and "que alimenta lloroso / el corazón" (23-4) for "que alimento lloroso." The suffering for love, however, is more explicit and accompanied by a personal cry of grief in the second version: "y la llama atrevida / que Amor, ¡triste de mí! arde en mis venas" (26-7) compared to the almost unstated idea of the first version: "aquel cuidado...que alimento lloroso / en abrasadas venas" (25, 27-8). Also the later version shows a tendency to more colloquial speech, using "negra sepultura" (32) in place of "triste sepultura."

The poem begins with a bold apostrophe to the hourglass, asking what is there to count since life is so short, a simple breath of life in which the whole journey is a single day. The characteristics of life suggest the workings of the timepiece. The journey of life is "breve y estrecha" like the neck of the glass, it goes from one pole to the other as the sands pass from one bulb to another, and it is a single "paso," just as the sands fall in one continuous movement. The next question uses the sands in the hourglass to contrast the shortness of life with the magnitude of suffering. Even though the timepiece can easily count out his life, it would be impossible to count his sufferings, even if the glass could hold as much sand

144

as the ocean bed. This comparison ingeniously suggests his tears are more numerous than the waters of the ocean. He finishes the first section, saying he does not want to hear, feel, or war against the passage of time, for eternity is sufficient time to meditate on death.

The next section returns to the theme of the brevity of life, saying that if the hourglass must measure his life span, it can rest soon, for the affairs of love and passion bring on death more quickly and shorten the duration of life. The last part of the poem is exactly the same in both versions, showing extreme concision and expression. The journey of life is now a pilgrimage in which the poet with sore feet circles the final goal, "la negra sepultura"(32), an image suggesting the ring of sand left in the upper globe of the hourglass as the center falls through the hole. Likewise, the poet will fall to his final doom in his final "paso."

The final five lines draw even more comparisons between the counter of time and the metaphysical existence of man. The "aliento fugitivo" (33) recalls the "soplo de vida" (2), the second phrase suggesting the Platonic soul's exile from paradise, seeking refuge in the fragility of the human body until such time as it is freed and can return to its true residence. And in the final comparison he sees the image of the human body and its life and death in that of the hourglass. If he dies, he will be like dust, and if he lives, his existence will be fragile, like the glass.

This poem treats a number of typical Quevedan themes: the brevity of life, the cares of life, the passion of love as consuming that life, the fragility of the body, and the pilgrimage of life and love. He makes his point by drawing comparisons from the central image of the hourglass. Rather than superficial and seemingly arbitrary, these comparisons, such as the brevity of life in

145

the quickness of the movement, the torment in the sands containing the unruly seas, the hole as sepulcher or final goal, and the fragility of man's existence in the sand and glass of the instrument that measures the extent of his life, bring forth subtle observations on man's existence that strike the reader as profound insights into the human dilemma.

Torre y Sevil combined the image of the sundial and the hourglass into a series of conceits portraying the lover's condition:

MIRA UN AMANTE, CIFRADO SU AMOR EN DOS RELOJES, UNO DE SOL, OTRO DE ARENA

Este, que en negras índices se explaya,
y en curso de las horas tiene a raya,
es seña de mi vida en sus desmayos;
Anarda, el bello sol; las rayas, rayos.
Este, en quien vierten con instancia llena,
dos nubes de cristal, lluvia de arena,
de mi abrasado amor, seña es gallarda,
mi pecho, el polvo; y el cristal, Anarda.
Y en fin, cuando infeliz mi amor me asombra,
si el uno lluvia es, y el otro es sombra,
a todas horas pintan mis enojos,
que uno es mi corazón, otro es mis ojos.[12]

The poem is based on a series of far-fetched comparisons that build to form an idea of the lover's suffering. His mistress, because of her luminous beauty, is the sun that illuminates the dial, and the dark lines, "rayas," showing the hours, are lightning flashes, "rayos," that produce his swooning. The "Anarda = sol" comparison is an archetype, but here serves in the specific context of the sundial. The "rayas = rayos" comparison is one of opposites, the shadow compared to lightning, based on

---

[12] *Varias hermosas flores del Parnaso* (Valencia: Francisco Mestre, 1680), 148.

an equivoque. The image of the hourglass further develops the suffering of the lover. The two glass bulbs which pour sand from one to the other are the mistress, and the sand that passes from one to the other is his bosom. The word "instancia" seems to be a play on the insistent passing of time and the word "instante," the moments which are marked by the flow of sand. The constant movement of the sand and the implicit association of "lluvia" and weeping make just the comparison of the sand to his breast. "Cristal" was a standard metaphor for the complexion of the lady, and hence is so used here to compare her to the hourglass. Since he compares the sand to his chest, the parallel comparison of the shape of the glass bulbs to the breasts of the lady is probably implicit, and quite typical of this type of *conceptismo*.

In the final comparison, if one timepiece is rain and the other shadow, then the shadow represents his dark heart and the rainfall his eyes. The imagery serves as the basis of a series of far-fetched conceits of the type that achieved great popularity in the poetry of Ledesma, but has generally been rejected by later periods as false comparisons and in bad taste. One imagines even the most generous of today's readers shuddering or groaning in response to the comparison of the glass bulbs to the breasts of the lady, or the word play "rayos = rayas." The reason for the adverse reaction lies in the fact that the image lacks a conceptual correspondence. The glass bulbs may resemble breasts, but the comparison in reality teaches us nothing about the nature of glass bulbs or breasts. The comparison seems to exist for its own sake. In contrast, Quevedo's imagery may produce a shock, but one that is a revelation of a new idea or hidden aspect of human existence. To see in the sand and glass a reminder of man's mortality, both his disintegration

147

after death and his fragile health in life, is a profound observation on the human condition. The fact that the passage of time is linked with man's mortality not only gives meaning to the comparison, but also gives it a sense of rightness that is aesthetically pleasing as well as conceptually profound. Quevedo's conceit produces several levels of contemplation, whereas Torre y Sevil's image of the two lovers in the hourglass is closed and limited to the surface meaning of the comparison. Even Owen's brief epigram which distorts reality by making the hole of the hourglass grow in size does so in order to make a point about the perception of time. Thus, even though he falsifies the truth, he realizes a higher psychological truth. It is precisely this higher truth that is missing from Torre y Sevil's comparison of the lovers to the sundial and hourglass. The poem consists of a series of improbable visual comparisons that ultimately do no more than display a rather insubstantial wit.

9. The Mechanical Clock

The image of the mechanical clock not only shows the same dichotomy between true and false wit, but also the development of certain themes, several of which become set poetic topics. More than any other mechanical device, the image of the clock is separated into well-defined thematic entities, such as religious themes, the clock illuminated by a candle, the lover and psychological time, and the clock as a moral emblem of good government.[1]

The clock in Baroque poetry is seldom a simple mechanical image analogous to some other operation. Almost always the concept of fleeting measured time and an impending threat of death lies menacingly behind the image. The poets often capitalize on the names of the parts of the clock to complete some aspect of the idea or image, such as "ruedas," "muestra," "pesas," "cuerda," "caja," "campana," "mano" and "espía," the wheel that brings in the chord or chain.

The mechanical clock is the only true machine that will be considered in this study. The compasses and scales are instruments for measuring, and even though the clock measures time, it is, with its weight-driven wheels, a machine that functions independently of the

---

[1] I omit The theme of the clock and the candle which has been treated by R. M. Price, ("The Lamp and the Clock: Quevedo's Reaction to a Commonplace," *MLN,* 82 [1967], 198-209). While it would be possible to add more examples to his study, he has already discussed the best example, Quevedo's sonnet, and few insights could be added to his observations.

time it measures. The conception of the universe as a giant machine found in the clock, with its various interdependent wheels, the perfect analogy for the even-paced nearly spherical movements of the planets. In fact, early clock-makers constructed mechanical representations of the universe using clock drives (Montañez, 1964: 104).

Little is known of the use of clocks in Spain before the introduction of the mechanical cathedral clock late in the fourteenth century. Alfonso X el Sabio's *Libros de saber de astronomía* (ca. 1265) explain the construction of different types of clocks. This treatise, the first in a modern European language to treat the construction of clocks, introduces from oriental and Arabic sources several types of clocks that are no longer used at all, such as the water and mercury clock (Montañez, 8-9). The use of weight-driven wheels to measure time was proposed about the middle of the thirteen century, but the necessary escapement to control the movement of the wheels was not invented until later in the same century (Fraser, 1975: 58-60).

Church documents show that mechanical clocks were installed on Cathedral towers from the late fourteenth century onwards: Valencia and Tortosa (built by Johannes Alemanus), 1378; Burgos, 1384; Palma de Mallorca, 1386, Lérida, 1390; Barcelona, 1393; and Seville, 1396.[2] These clocks typically were twenty-four hour weight-driven clocks with only one hand indicating the hour. They also chimed the hour, and at times the quarter hour. They were not very accurate and the sundial and hourglass continued to be used. In fact over a half dozen treatises on the construction of the sundial

---

[2] The list is compiled from Montañez Fontenla, 61, and Fernando Landeira de Compostela, *Theatro chronométrico del noroeste español* (Madrid: Roberto Carbonell, 1957), 6.

had appeared before the publication of the first treatise on clock-making in 1759 (Montañez, 1964: 18). The spring drive was introduced at the end of the fifteenth century, but the clock did not become reliable for long periods of time until the invention of the pendulum escape drive in the mid-seventeenth century (Crombie, 1959: 98). Charles V employed a clock maker, the famous Gianelli della Torre, or known in Spain as Juanelo Turriano. He is most often remembered in Golden Age literature as the inventor of the "ingenio," the machine for raising water to the city of Toledo. He designed and built numerous mechanical devices, and left a notebook of drawings and plans. He followed Charles V into retirement at Yuste where he continued to build numerous machines, including a very elaborate astronomical clock (Montañez, 1964: 104).

Even though clocks were introduced in private houses at the beginning of the sixteenth century (Herrero García, 1955: 27), and the first mention of a pocket watch is as early as 1469 (Ibid., 47), the accuracy of small mechanical clocks did not supersede that of other clocks until the eighteenth century. An evaluation of these clocks is found in a late sixteenth-century discourse:

> Son los hombres en la trabazón del cuerpo humano como los relojes entre los cuales hay unos de campanario, otros de mesa y pared y otros de pecho. Estos últimos se desconciertan tan a menudo que han menester la hacienda de un honrado clérigo para entretenellos.... Pero los otros, que a todas horas están sobre las torres eminentes, sin rehuir los combates de las lluvias, las baterías de los aires, los asoleos de los rayos y finalmente los golpes de un continuo martillo, muy a tarde se desconciertan....[3]

---

[3] Daniel L. Heiple, "'El apellido *pícaro* se deriua de *picar.*' Nueva documentación sobre su etimología," in *La picaresca. Orígienes, textos y estructuras,* ed. Manuel Criado de Val (Madrid: Fundación Universitaria Española, 1979), 217-230.

According to Santos Torroella (1953: 3), the first poem in Spanish to treat the image of the clock is a riddle by Juan de Mena:

XOLER

¿Qué es el cuerpo sin sentido
que concierta nuestras vidas
    sin vivir,
muévese sin ser movido,
hace cosas muy sentidas
    sin sentir.
Este nunca está dormido,

mas siempre mide medidas
    sin medir;
tiene el seso tan perdido
que el mismo se da heridas
    sin herir?

The poem consists of a number of ingenious oxymora based on conceptual contrasts between the movement of the clock and its lifelessness. Associating animation with life, the poet plays on the paradox that the clock has many lifelike functions but remains lifeless. It moves without feeling movement or being moved emotionally, creates anguish at passing time without feeling, measures without measuring anything spatially visible, and, in a final pun, strikes without injuring itself. This poem is typical of fifteenth-century *conceptismo* with its abstract word plays and repetition of different forms of the same word (mide, medidas, medir). Even though this *conceptismo* survived into the seventeenth century, as seen in two riddles of Cristóbal Pérez de Herrera (Santos Torroella, 1953: 6-7), the two types of *conceptismo* are completely different. Seventeenth-century poetic language is more concrete and sensual, and the paradox often lies implicit in the image rather than constituting the substance. The combination of reiterated conceptual play, the intellectual language, and tautness of construction of this poem create a completely different style from most of the poems analyzed in this study.

The Allegorical Clock

One category of poems consists of extravagant religious allegories based on the mechanics of the clock parts. Using paradoxes like those of Mena and Pérez de Herrera, these poems point their far-fetched comparisons to religious allegories, such as Torre y Sevil's sonnet to a clock decorated with a statue of Christ tied to the column. The juxtaposition of the clock and the statue provides an accidental correlation for which the poet attempts to discover the witty correspondence that placed them together:

A CHRISTO EN UN RELOJ, ATADO A LA COLUNA,
SIN LOS MINISTROS DE LOS AZOTES

¿Quién a coluna, y a reloj te auna,
Señor? ¿Si es porque espíritu es tu aliento,
y en la rueda del tiempo fraudulento
de mi error, la constancia es la coluna?
En el sangriento horror, que te importuna,
y en el artificioso movimiento,
mis culpas contaré de ciento en ciento,
cuando mido las horas de una en una.
¿Pero cómo en el mármol te comprendo,
cuando con rosicler su espacio doras,
sin los ministros del afán horrendo?
Mas, ¡ay!, que el reloj suple iras traidoras,
que como a todas horas yo te ofendo,
son azotes los golpes de las horas.

                         (Oven, 1674: 227)

He sees in the combination of the *Ecce Homo* and the clock three possible correspondences: (1) the seemingly effortless movement of the clock suggests that it is driven by Christ's invisible spirit, (2) the deceptive nature of time suggests the hollowness of sin, and (3) the firmness of the column represents the persistency of his erring ways. He continues to develop the comparison of sin to time, specifically comparing sin to the hours. The accidental correlation is based on an equivoque on the unstated Spanish verb "herir," which means to strike the hour, but whose primary meaning is to wound. This pun provides the basis of a conceptual correspondence of function. Even though a hundred times more numerous, his sins are like the hours struck on the clock because they continually strike and injure the person of Christ. He continues to develop the image, assuming that the agents of torture are not physically portrayed in the statue because, personified by the striking of the hour, they are present in the juxtaposed clock. Like sin, the hours are flagellants that continue to torture Christ. The poet ingeniously moralizes the relationship of the statue and clock by seeing the striking of the hour as the flagellation of Christ—each chime of the clock is like a hundred blows delivered by a hundred sins, which are as constant in man's life as the column to which Christ is bound. Even though the invisibility of time is compared to the hollowness of sin, the poet is not as interested in exploring the nature of time as he is in displaying his ingenuity by extracting a moral reading from the emblem of the "Ecce homo" placed next to a clock.

In a similar vein, but even more extravagant are the poet's four *décimas* dedicated to a clock with porcelain figures of the Holy Family. Like the previous poem, the allegory deals with the statues in relation to time:

154

Reloj, que culto arrebol
también retrato te nombra,
tres soles, te hacen de sombra,
tres sombras, te hacen de sol,
luz en Josef, fiel crisol;
sol en Jesus atesoras;
y alba, en María; mejoras
de un reloj que une a porfías,
el acierto de los días,
y el concierto de las horas.

Si das vuelta a tu fortuna,
y cuentas las horas, es
María en gracia, las tres,
pero entre todas, la una.
De reloj joya oportuna,
cajuela, Josef será,
y Jesus mi metal; ya
la campanilla no tarda,
Josef, porque es el que guarda,
Jesus, porque es el que da.

Saetilla, fiel medida
también en Jesus se advierte,
que en tres horas de su muerte,
siglos señala a mi vida.
Rueda en fortuna subida
Josef es, y entre los dos,
la cuerda, ¡O María!, vos,
que mueve en veloz agrado,
sin el peso del pecado,
el Espíritu de Dios.

Virgen, si cuerda lo atento
os mira, mi juicio atad,
Josef, si sois rueda, dad
a mis pasos movimiento:
y si campanilla os siento,
¡O Jesus!, palabra y son,
pues en el reloj mansión
de vos a mi pecho he hecho,

155

cuando toquéis en el pecho,
tocadme en el corazón.

(*Varias hermosas flores,* 1680: 25-6)

The poet compares the members of the Holy Family to various parts of the clock. First they are compared to light; and then Mary becomes the hours and the chain or chord, Joseph the case that holds the clock and a wheel, and Jesus the chime and the hand. Most of these comparisons are established through equivocal correlations which lack a conceptual correspondence. In some cases, the poet extracts further correlations from other word plays. In the first *décima,* he compares the figures with the sun, calling them three suns that cast three shadows. Since the clock lies in shadows, it is a sundial. The image "mechanical clock = sundial" has no real deeper meaning than the play of words involved. Each of the figures represents an aspect of the sun (correlations, except for the first, based on archetypal ideas): Joseph is the light, a faithful receptacle; Jesus is the treasure of the sun, i.e. gold; and Mary the dawn, a traditional comparison. He establishes a further comparison by maintaining that the clock with its statues is superior because it joins the message of the days with the harmony of the hours. The word plays are indeed specious. "Acierto" is correlated with "concierto" through sound similarity. Both words serve as points of correspondence between the clock and the Holy Family. The "acierto de los días" joins the two by referring to the time-telling function of the clock and the eternal message of the Holy Family, and the "concierto de las horas" links them by referring to the harmony of the clock mechanism and the conformity of the Holy Family with the divine plan.

In the second stanza, the poet establishes new images by providing new figures based on equivoques. Mary is

156

compared to the times of the day, Joseph to the clock case, and Jesus to the chimes. The face of the clock is like a wheel of Fortune, and as it turns it shows Mary to be three (o'clock) in grace, and first among all. The image of Joseph as the clock case (recalling that he was a carpenter and a craftsman) lacks a conceptual correspondence and has only the accidental correlation based on an equivoque on the word "guardar." Since he suffered patiently Mary's giving birth, he is the one who waits ("guarda"), and hence is like the clock case which guards the clock. The comparison of Jesus to the chime of the clock is based on two separate images. In the first, the accidental correlation is established through a equivoque on "dar": Jesus gives salvation as the chime strikes ("da") the hour. And in the second the hardness of the metal chime is a similitude for man's spiritual strength. In neither image is the conceptual correspondence well developed, showing Torre y Sevil's preference for the decorative conceit.

In the next stanza, the poet takes up three new comparisons which he resolves in the final stanza. Jesus is compared to the pointer which faithfully measures time, for the three hours of his Passion signified the gift of eternal salvation to man. Joseph is compared to the high point of the wheel of fortune without an explanation of the correlation. And finally, Mary is the chain or cord suspending the weights that drive the mechanism. The position of the word "cuerda": "la cuerda, ¡O María!, vos," allows it to be both the cord of the clock and a substantivized adjective meaning the sane person. Torre y Sevil then develops a further conceit on the comparison by having the cord moved by the Holy Spirit, free from the weight of sin, a correlation based on opposition of function. It is a lack of weight that drives the clock and allows the conceit. The freedom from sin refers both to

157

the spiritual nature of the love between God and the Virgin and also to the Immaculate Conception, the dogma by which Mary was conceived without original sin.

The last stanza completes the comparisons from the previous two stanzas, and develops further word plays from them. If the Virgin is the cord of the clock, then she should curb (bind) his judgment. If Joseph is the wheel, then he should move and direct the poet's steps to God. And if Jesus is the chime, then let him sound out and have His voice lead us. The final conceit argues that if the clock is the abode of Jesus and he makes of his bosom a resting place for it, then when the chime sounds (toquéis) in Christ's chest, let it affect the poet (tocadme) in his heart and feeling. Torre y Sevil, through a series of puns, extracts an extravagant moral reading from the emblem of a clock graced by figures of the Holy Family.

Torre y Sevil's "conceptismo" in these poems is very much like the style introduced by Alonso de Ledesma at the beginning of the seventeenth century. His *Conceptos espirituales y morales* (1606) were extremely popular, but have been labeled since as false wit and in poor taste by critics who maintain that poetry should express natural thoughts. Among Ledesma's *Conceptos* is a *villancico* which sees the nativity in the works of the clock. The poem consists of an *estribillo* of two parts: a three-line introduction followed by a five-line refrain which is repeated as the second half of each *décima*.

Pr. A, señores, ¿qué hora es,
que parece medio día?
Resp. A hora de Santa María,
una, dos, hombre y Dios;
tres, de las tres personas es,
que el amor sin duda alguna
a las doce dio la una
y en el cielo son las tres.

En la torre de San Juan
está la mano clavada,
en la una que es ya dada
para el rescate de Adán,
dan, a Dios nos dan,
una, dos, hombre y Dios;
tres, de las tres personas es,
que el amor sin duda alguna
a las doce dio la una,
y en el cielo son las tres.
    Este reloj no había
cuartos de hora, pero ya
todos cuatro cuartos da
el reloj Santa María.
Contadlas bien alma mía,
una, dos, hombre y Dios;
tres, de las tres personas es,
que el amor sin duda alguna,
a las doce dio la una,
y en el cielo son las tres.[4]

The first part of the estribillo asks the time, and the
response in the refrain says it is the time of the Virgin (the
hour when she gave birth), it is both one and two,
representing the union of the integers one and two in
Christ as both man and God, and it is three because of
the three persons of the Trinity. So at twelve, the
moment of the Nativity, the clock struck one and two for
the Incarnation of God in man, and three for the persons
of the Trinity. In the first *copla,* the hand of the clock is
nailed to the one of the Incarnation as Christ's hand will
be nailed to the cross in ransoming man from Adam's
sin, with the repetition of "dan" representing the striking
of the bell. The second *copla* introduces the number
four, claiming the clock that strikes the quarter hour was
introduced with the Virgin Mary. This is a fine example

[4] Alonso de Ledesma, *Conceptos espirituales y morales,* II, ed. Eduardo
Julia Martínez (Madrid: CSIC, 1969), 30-1.

(no matter how simplistic) of Ledesma's *conceptismo,* a far-fetched allegory transposing the times on the clock into the essential mysteries of the Nativity: the Incarnation of God into the human figure of Christ and the Unity of the Godhead in the Trinity.

Lope de Vega imitated this poem in his pastoral novel *Los pastores de Belén.* The poem consists of an *estribillo* followed by two *coplas,* the first half of each one is a *redondilla* and the second half an *estribillo* utilizing the rhyme words of Ledesma's poem:

> Un reloj he visto, Andrés,
> que sin verse rueda alguna
> *que en el suelo da la una,*
>
> *siendo en el cielo las tres.*
>   ¡Oh, qué bien has acertado,
> porque de las tres del cielo
> hoy la segunda en el suelo
> para bien del hombre ha dado!
> Con las ruedas que no ves,
> porque está secreta alguna,
> *en el suelo da la una,*
> *siendo en el cielo las tres.*
>   Este reloj, que sustenta
> cielo y tierra, es tan sutil,
> que, con dar una, da mil
> mercedes a quien las cuenta;
> cuenta las horas, Andrés,
> y di sin errar ninguna
> *que en el suelo da la una,*
> *siendo en el cielo las tres.*[5]

Lope's poem makes the same point as Ledesma's, but is more clearly focused. The *estribillo* uses the clock image to repeat as hours of the day two different mysteries: Christ's Incarnation, "en el suelo da la una," and the Trinity, "siendo en el cielo las tres." Essentially, Lope's

---

[5]   Lope de Vega, *Los pastores de Belén,* 1467b.

imitation eliminates unnecessary comparisons, adding clarity and direction, and therefore seems less diffuse and rambling.

In all four of these poems, the authors allegorize the clock, its parts, and the hours into some aspect of religious dogma. Characteristic of Ledesma's *conceptismo,* none of the comparisons in these poems shows more than a momentarily fleeting association, and hence does not lead to a deeper perception of reality or reveal an inner truth. When Quevedo says the moments are interred in our body, "cada instante en el cuerpo sepultada" (Quevedo, 1963: 11), he is presenting a fundamental truth about aging: man is essentially linked to time and the passing (death) of each moment accumulates into the weight of one's age, so that in some real sense, man is the burial ground for time. No such perception is reached in the four poems treated here. Twelve, one, two, and three o'clock have no real connection with the nativity, nor do the comparisons deepen our understanding of time or the Incarnation. Likewise, Christ tied to the column does not have an intrinsic relationship to time, nor are the members of the Holy Family related to clock parts. The neo-classicists had harsh words for the Baroque habit of departing from natural comparisons. Dr. Johnson said of this falsity: "whatever is improper or vicious is produced by a voluntary deviation from nature in pursuit of something new and strange, and ... the writers fail to give delight by their desire of exciting imagination" (Johnson, 1967: 35). Only in the present century have some critics been able to divorce themselves from the harsh strictures of post-Baroque criticism and come to a limited appreciation of this poetry. Even so, the dichotomy established by the Neo-Classical precept that metaphors must adhere to nature still survives in our evaluation of

161

these works. Since the sign and figure have no real relationship, the four poems do not seem to fit in this study, and even though they name parts of clocks, they are not about clocks or mechanics. It seems that any comparison would have served as long as it displayed the poet's wit, and a survey of the table of contents of Ledesma's poetry shows that he indeed used many improbable metaphors. This category of clock poems is not about science at all, but consists of far-fetched religious allegories.

Time and the Lover's Anxiety

The clock and anxiety of passing time became a metaphor in the *comedia* for the lover's anxieties. Oftentimes the poet sees in the hours on the face of the clock the influence of the twelve astrological signs, and, because of his suffering, he distinguishes real time from the psychological perception of time. In a concise and excellent image from *El burlador de Sevilla,* Batricio, as he impatiently awaits Aminta, who is with don Juan, compares his jealousy to a clock:

> Celos, reloj de cuidados,
> que a todas las horas dais
> tormentos con que matáis,
> aunque dais desconcertados. (*Diez comedias*, 289)

The image of a clock as jealousy is based on an antithesis, since there is no real accidental correlation between them. Conceptually, jealousy is a clock because both represent anxiety over loss: time as the inescapable passing of life and loss of self and jealousy as the helpless feeling of losing a loved person. The justness of the comparison arises from the similarity of man's emotional response to both situations. Tirso extends the comparison by saying that as a clock constantly gives or strikes the hour, so does jealousy create constant torments. The final touch is produced by a contrast. A well adjusted clock (concertado) will give the hour regularly, but since the torments of jealousy unbalance one's emotional stability, he labels the lover's torments as "desconcertados." This brief comparison, which enhances the rich texture of Tirso's masterpiece, very aptly and concisely characterizes jealousy by comparing it to the anguish felt at passing time.

In *La dama boba,* Lope's protagonist uses the imperceptible movement of the hand of the clock from one hour to another to explain his change of heart:

> ¿No has visto que saeta
> del reloj en un lugar
> firme siempre suele estar
> aunque nunca está quieta,
> y tal vez está en la una,
> y luego en las dos está?
> Pues, así mi alma ya,
> sin hacer mudanza alguna
> de la casa en que me ves
> desde Nise que ha querido,
> a las doce se ha subido,
> que es número de interés.[6]

Again one notes in Lope a surprising attention to observable detail which becomes the correlation of an

---

[6] Lope de Vega, *La dama boba,* ed. Alonso Zamora Vicente (Madrid: Clásicos Castellanos, 1963), 173-4. A similar observation is found in *El perro del hortelano:* "¿No has visto faltar la cuerda / de un reloj, y estarse quedas / sin movimiento las ruedas?" Lope de Vega, *Obras,* XIII, ed. Emilio Cotarelo y Mori (Madrid: RAE, 1930), 209b.

image. The hero notes that the hand of the clock cannot be seen to move, but in fact actually does move from one number to the other. He claims that he once preferred Nise, but slowly he has had a change of heart just as the hand of a clock can be seen pointing at one o'clock and without being seen to move later points at two. The word "casa" plays on the fact that the "galán" remains in the same house in Madrid, in the same family, and also in the same astrological "house" or sign. The "número de interés" is a further cosmological reference based on the fact that some angles between signs were considered favorable to love, namely the angles of 60° and 120°, while others were in opposition, namely 180° and 90°. The indicator of his love has imperceptibly shifted until he is at an angle favorable to Finea rather than Nise. Lope has employed an image of the clock based on close observation of detail and, by extension, he converts it into an astrological clock showing inclinations and disaffections governing a lover's passion.

In Calderón's *La señora y la criada,* Diana receives a watch from an admirer,and when alone, she addresses it:

> Basilisco del tiempo, tú que doras
> con la tez hoy del oro y los diamantes
> el veneno que a todos por instantes
> da la muerte, que a todos das por horas,
>
> ¿cómo el punto que muestras ése ignoras,
> pues no abrevias aquél en que inconstantes
> influyen su rigor astros amantes?
> Pero cuéntaslos tú, no los mejoras.
>
> Si la casa de Venus terminada
> quieres saber, ¡oh sabia astrología!,
> yo en un reloj la tengo señalada.
>
> Tu astrolabio será la suerte mía;
> mira en mí, y el de un alma enamorada,
> el minuto, el instante, la hora, el día.
>
> (Calderón, 1960: II, 847b)

The octave is addressed to the timepiece, contrasting the deadliness of the message to the indifference with which the clock delivers it. The basilisk is a semimythical reptile that supposedly gave forth venom with its look. She sees in the time of the clock a slow poison opulently gilded and decorated with jewels. As typical in Calderón, the language is far more subtle than it appears on first impression. In the first two lines, "dorar la tez del oro" refers to the clock case, but the personification in "tez" also suggests the blonde hair of youth. The watch is richly decorated, as is youth which will pass. The awkward placement of "hoy" calls attention to the word and suggests it is out of place and mutable. Lines 3 and 4 seem to be parallel with the same stressed syllables falling on the same phrase "que a todos" in both lines, and forming an assonant rhyme with "del oro" from the stressed syllables of line two, but the parallelism is broken in the phrases "por instantes" and "por horas." The meaning of "por" changes from the first to second phrase. In the first example, "el veneno que a todos por instantes da la muerte," suggests a poison that is given every instant, but in the second phrase, "que a todos das por horas" suggests the reading "as hours," that the "horas" are in effect the substance of the poison. The first quatrain presents time as a slow ceaseless poison that is dispensed from a gilded case, and even though it may favor us with youth today, it will slowly and surely destroy us.

The second quatrain constrasts psychological time with regulated time. She claims the clock must not realize the import of its message, or it would otherwise shorten the time that one must suffer under the torments of love. The reference to the stars and their inconstant influence recalls the effect of suffering, and how it stretches out the feeling of time. The clock only counts, it does not alleviate suffering. The first quatrain presents the effects of passing time on all mankind, but the second quatrain suggests that certain times, especially the tormented anxiety of love, should be accelerated.

While the octave is addressed to the clock, the sextet picks up the star image from line 7, and is addressed to astrology. Since the watch was a lover's gift, she sees in it the greatest influence of the star of love. "Términos" in astrology refer to those degrees in which the star has its maximum influence. In the final image, her fortunes in love will be the astrolabe of astronomy used for determining the position of a star. The accidental correlation is an equivoque, based on "minuto" and "hora" which are measured by the clock and also used to indicate the degrees of the position of a star. Conceptually, since the clock as a lover's gift exerts astral influences on her, and since it measures the minutes and hours, it is an astrolabe indicating the position of the planet of love.

The watch has undergone several subtle transformations, from a venomous reptile to an instrument for measuring the position and effect of the stars. More importantly, the clock and the regularity of its action create an irregular effect, increasing the bond of love and paradoxically stretching out the time of torment. Thus, love and torment produce a new concept: the psychological sense of the passage of time.

Lope de Vega in his pastoral novel *La Arcadia* brings out clearly the effect of psychological time created by love. In the *décimas* dedicated to the watch given him by his beloved, Menalca sees it as an emblem: "la impresa de mis porfías."[7] The regularity of the clock reminds

---

[7] Lope de Vega, *La Arcadia,* ed. Edwin S. Morby (Madrid: Clásicos Castalia, 1975), 290-2.

him how long the suffering of love seems, how each hour becomes years:

> reloj de las horas mías,
> que paso sin vos, señora,
> el índice de mis daños,
> cuenta despacio los años
> de un hora que el alma llora. (290)

He distinguishes two different kinds of time, that experienced by the lover and that given by the clock:

> Poco mi tormento impiden
> tus horas de tiempo llenas,
> pues no se miden las penas
> como las horas se miden;
> éstas el tiempo dividen,
> sus partes mostrando al tiempo
> que el humano pasatiempo
> pasa el tiempo en esta calma;
> pero las horas del alma
> no se miden con el tiempo.
> Si lo que paso sintieses,
> reloj, en tan largos días,
> más apriesa pasarías
> horas que ausente me vieses;
> yo aseguro que corrieses
> tan ligero por mi vida,
> que al margen de su corrida
> llegases en un momento;
> pero la pena que siento,
> no hay pena con que se mida. (291)

Distinct from the fantastic religious allegories of Torre y Sevil and Ledesma are the poems on time and love which place emphasis on time as an astral influence inclining one to love and creating a tormented suffering that seems to lengthen the hours. These poems seem more realistic because the comparisons, even though forced and based on contrived correlations, present the reality of man's psychological state while in torment. Like the

167

shepherd's in the pastoral poems who viewed themselves as alienated from time, the lover sees the irregularity of his passionate suffering as setting him aside from measured time, extending his torments into a long drawn-out state of anxiety that dilates the concept of time.

The Clock as Moral Emblem

The following group of poems is similar to the earlier group of far-fetched conceits in that in both types of poem the poet takes a message from the workings of the clock. The earlier group, however, established elaborate allegorical conceits whose points of reference were more or less arbitrary. The following selection of poems differs in that while it makes elaborate comparisons based on the clock, it looks to the metaphysical and moral character of man's existence, hence time is part of the basic metaphor. In these poems, the clock is not simply the point of departure for a series of far-fetched comparisons, but stands for fleeting time, and presents the problem of man's reconciliation to this world. The theme of "desengaño" playing a substantial role in these poems. Parting from the theme of morality as regulation of the passions, the poems become more philosophical and less didactic, playing incessantly on the metaphysical paradoxes of existence.

Covarrubias' Emblema 42 from Book II pictures a weight-driven clock with the paradoxical motto "pondere levior," you will weigh more lightly. The clock has one hand, as was typical of clocks in that period, and its face is mounted backwards, which may be an engraver's error. The top of the case is mounted with a hemisphere of a globe and is carried in the air by a pair of wings, apparently trying to deceive the interpreter into concluding beforehand that the emblem teaches him that "time flies." The poem takes its message from two aspects of the clock: (1) the paradox that it functions more swiftly the heavier its weights, and (2) the fact it is constant in its workings:

> Anda el reloj de pesas más ligero,
> cuando ellas son más graves y pesadas;
> el hombre cuanto más grave y entero,
> tanto más asegura sus pisadas,
> ágil, firme, constante y verdadero,
> señalando sus horas compasadas;
> en fin es un reloj tan regulado
> que tarde o nunca está desconcertado.
>   (Covarrubias, 1610: 142)

The prose commentary explains that this is an emblem for governors and rulers. While they should act with gravity and ponder issues carefully, that should not be a pretext for delaying justice, but rather, like the clock, the added weight should make it function more quickly and, like time, take on wings of diligence. Although Covarrubias does not make explicit the basis of the image, undoubtedly the comparison takes its starting point from the clock's perfect regularity—a perfection in the art of governing which can serve as an example for man's actions.

López de Zárate used the image of the clock in a sonnet as double emblematic motif, teaching both the value of time and clemency:

169

ENSEÑANDO A UN PRINCIPE EN UN RELOJ
A APROVECHAR EL TIEMPO, Y A SER BENIGNO

Pues tu centro es el índice, que ajusta
peso, y reloj, en éste que señala
las horas, las distingue, las iguala,
haz con su imitación tu fama Augusta.
    Pase a la zona opuesta de la adusta
el sol; verás que si, fecundando, exhala,
volviendo al campo lo que ardiendo tala;
que la razón más blanda, es la más justa.
    Muéstranse sus minutos, sus instantes
a grandes y menores, porque vean
que aun el tiempo es a cargo de los reyes.
    Postrará peso tanto mil Athlantes:
mas que brazos con él no se recrean,
juzgándose colunas de las leyes!

(López de Zárate, 1947: II, 260)

The poem is addressed to the ruler, "el príncipe," a title hallowed by both the Machiavellian and Anti-Machiavellian traditions. The first point of comparison of the ruler to the clock involves two equivoques on "centro" and "índice." The meanings of "centro" are so broad as to make it difficult to state succinctly the figure, but the meanings of administrative center or point of attraction are suggested by the literal center of the face of the clock. These centers are the "índice," that is, the hand that points to the hour, as well as the index, or "indicio," of his activity. Since the prince's conduct and administration are an indicator, and since the hand of the clock indicates the hour, then the prince should imitate the clock whose hand is measured by weight and balance. He should see in the hand which points to the hours a point of comparison for achieving fame, since it distinguishes them and makes them equal. Typical of metaphysical style which plays with false symmetries, line 3 has six words divided into three parallel groups of two, each beginning with "las," but the symmetry is broken by one being a noun and the other two verbs.

In the second quatrain, the movement of the burning summer sun, undoubtedly conceived of as a cosmic clock circling the globe, is an example of destructive harshness, while the warm sun in a milder season is an image of fertility and the creation of life from the very ground that was devastated. These example demonstrate that a moderate rule is more productive than a harsh one. The prince should lead an open life, revealing every moment to show that he controls his life and time. The last tercet plays on the "arms of the law" for creating justice and the arms that sustain the weight of government. Like Atlas, the arms of the law become columns of support for the weight of governing. This poem stands midway between the poems that are purely moral in tone and those that, like the following ones by Quevedo and those attributed to Góngora, move into a more general moral, or even philosophical, message about man's existence.

Quevedo's *silva* to the mechanical chime clock plays incessantly on the contrast between the sweetness of the sound of the chime and the harshness of the message of passing time:

RELOJ DE CAMPANILLA

El metal animado,
a quien mano atrevida, industriosa,
secretamente ha dado
vida aparente en máquina preciosa,
organizando atento   5
sonora voz a docto movimiento;
en quien, desconocido
espíritu secreto, brevemente
en un orbe ceñido,
muestra el camino de la luz ardiente,   10
y con rueda importuna

los trabajos del sol y de la luna,
y, entre ocasos y auroras,
las peregrinaciones de las horas;
máquina en que el artífice, que pudo   15
contar pasos al sol, horas al día,
mostró más providencia que osadía,
fabricando en metal disimuladas
advertencias sonoras repetidas,
pocas veces creídas,   20
muchas veces contadas;
tú, que estás muy preciado
de tener el más cierto, el más limado,
con diferente oído,
atiende a su intención y a su sonido.   25
    La hora irrevocable que dio, llora;
prevén la que ha de dar; y la que cuentas,
lógrala bien, que en una misma hora
te creces y te ausentas.
Si le llevas curioso,   30
atiéndele prudente,
que los blasones de la edad desmiente;
y en traje de reloj llevas contigo,
del mayor enemigo,
espía desvelada y elegante,   35
a ti tan semejante,
que, presumiendo de abreviar ligera
la vida al sol, al cielo la carrera,
fundas toda esta máquina admirada
en una cuerda enferma y delicada,   40
que, como la salud en el más sano,
se gasta con sus ruedas y su mano.
    Estima sus recuerdos,
teme sus desengaños,
pues ejecuta plazos de los años,   45
y en él te da secreto,
a cada sol que pasa, a cada rayo,
la muerte un contador, el tiempo un ayo.
                    (Quevedo, 1963: 121-2)

He begins repeating the traditional play between the movement of the clock with its appearance of life and its actual lifelessness, synthesized in the oxymoron "metal animado." The clock has a "desconocido espíritu secreto" which allows it to measure the movement of the sun and moon, and the passing hours. In order to bring out the contradiction between the sonority of the chime and the grim reality of the message, he twice refers to the sweetness of the chime by repeating the adjective *sonoro:* "sonora voz" (6) and "advertencias sonoras repetidas" (19), although the last one is qualified as "disimuladas" (18), as he prepares for the theme of the unheeded passage of time. The chimes are more often counted than actually perceived, and he asks the reader to tune his ear to the intention of the chimes as well as their sound.

The suggestion of a deeper meaning in the sound of the chimes opens the way for the *desengaño.* One must mourn the passing hour and fulfill himself in the new one, for one by one they accumulate into the passing of an age. The announcement of the theme allows him to pun on a part of the clock. One carries in the case of the clock a spy from his greatest enemy. This is a pun on the word "espía," in its sense of the wheel that draws in the cord, and its sense of a secret agent of an enemy power. The "espía" never sleeps and always draws in the cord of time—man's greatest enemy before whom he will inevitably fall. He sees in the whole machine a sign for the human body, since the clock depends on a weak sickly cord, and its wheels and hands, like the health of man, wear out with time. Like other poets, especially Góngora, Quevedo sees in the clock the image of man, the machine that wears away with age and whose parts are susceptible to failure at any moment.

Quevedo exhorts his reader to listen to the chimes (recuerdos) and fear the moment of realizing the effects of time, for the chimes are a counter for death and a master for time. More so than the other *silvas* on clocks, this poem depends less on puns and clock parts, and delves more into the nature of time. The clock with its chimes may mark hourly the passage of time, but man may only hear the sweetness of the tone without realizing that it is sounding his impending doom. While he does pun on "espía," that allows him the opportunity to characterize further the nature of time as man's greatest enemy.

Among the *décimas* attributed to Góngora that describe different ways of telling time are four treating mechanical clocks: the needle and cord clock, the clock that strikes the quarter hour, the chime clock, and the pocket watch (de pecho). Each one is addressed to time and each makes, usually by contrasting the timepiece to the nature of time, a different point about man's paradoxical relation to time. The *décima* dedicated to the weight driven clock describes the clock as an image of time and of human life:

DE AGUJA Y CUERDA

En engaste de marfil
tu retrato, ¡oh tiempo ingrato!,
me sueles dar, si retrato
hay de cosa tan sutil;
una aguja en su viril,
él claro, ella inquieta,
así es tu imagen perfeta,
y la de mi vida amada,
una hebra delicada,
a tus mudanzas sujeta. (Góngora, 1961: 434)

The poet sees in the timepiece an image of time framed in ivory, if ever it were possible to portray time. The clock consists of a needle in a glass case; the needle is inconstant and the glass clear. It forms a perfect image

174

of time in relation to the poet's beloved life—a delicate thread subject to the movement of time.

The *décima* dedicated to the clock that chimes the quarter hour treats the theme of the brevity of life:

DE CUARTOS

Vida miserable en quien
nunca de ti estamos hartos:
¿por qué por puntos y cuartos
quieres, tiempo, que te den?
Pero medirte así es bien;
pues ya la experiencia enseña
(o vela la vida, o sueña)
que no con mayor medida
se dividirá una vida
tan invisible y pequeña. (Góngora, 1961, 435)

Since the "reloj de cuartos" was so unreliable and since the "cuarto" was a coin, which because of devaluation of the coinage, had negligible value, it makes an apt point of comparison for emphasizing the misery of man's existence. The poet complains that he never has enough time ("nunca de ti estamos hartos") and questions the purpose of marking the quarter hour. The answer is ironic: no matter how man spends his life, it is so short that it cannot be divided into larger divisions. Unlike the other "décimas," this poem is completely rhetorical, based on plain statement and rhetorical irony, instead of concrete imagery.

The *décima* on the bell tower clock treats psychological time, contrasting its real speed with its apparent speed:

DE CAMPANA

¿Qué importan, porque te estés,
tantas ruedas diferentes,
si, gastándote en sus dientes,
vas más ligero después?
¿Qué importa calzar tus pies
de plomo, en pesos, si habitas
el viento y te precipitas
con la pesadumbre más,
y a veces de metal das
lo que callando nos quitas? (Góngora, 1961: 434)

Addressed to time, the poem asks two rhetorical questions that characterize the flow of time. In both questions he uses the parts of the clock as signs indicating an attempt to check its speed. First he asks why hold back the movement of the clock with various wheels and escapes, when these with wear will only increase the speed of the clock. The obvious conclusion that any attempt to halt the flow of time will simply result in an apparent increase in the speed of time later. The second question makes the same point. It is based on a false analogy in which he sees the lead weights as an attempt to weigh down the speed of time, but then answers by revealing that the result of the added weights is to give movement to the clock. He asks why add lead weights to the feet of time, if time lives in the wind and with added weight only runs faster. He adds finally that since it is a bell clock, it occasionally sounds what is silently stolen from us. In this poem, the flow of time is gauged to the clock, and attempts to slow the clock only increase its speed later. Thus, man's efforts to control time are frustrated and counteracted by natural forces.

The *décima* on the pocket watch deals with the illusory speed of time:

PARA EL PECHO

Tal vez en paredes de oro
te vi encerrado, y allí
armado también te vi
contra el pecho en que te honoro.
Siempre eres, tiempo, tesoro;
pero, dime, ¿qué aprovecha
encerrarte en caja estrecha
y envolverte en oro, pues
huyes, tiempo, y, parto, ves,
huyendo, [a] alcanzar tu flecha? (Góngora, 1961: 436)

Addressed to time itself, the poem presents it as enclosed
in a golden cage, but even so it is armed (the arrow that
indicates the hour) against its bearer. Developing the
image of time stored in a gold box, he imagines it as a
stored and protected treasure, but then questions how
time, eternally fleeing, can be stored and stopped. Since
it flees, he too will flee, hoping to catch the "flecha."
This last word is purposely ambiguous in order to evoke
the hand of the clock marking the passing hour, the speed
of an arrow representing the swiftness of time, and,
finally, the weapons of time armed against man. The
arrow of time, either as the hand of a clock or the speed
of fleeting time, is a deadly assassin armed against the
poet, who proudly displays his watch, unaware of the
dangers held in the golden treasure case, or of the
impossibility of caging time.

The unusual aspect of these *décimas* is their treatment
of time as an abstract philosophical question. Most
treatments of the clock and time concentrate on man's
personal involvement, whereas these short epigrammatic
poems show more interest in the philosophical paradoxes
of the invisibility and inevitability of the passage of time,
while at the same time having to face its effects. They are
masterful little poems of a kind that is quite unusual in

177

the Spanish Golden Age, and worthy of more attention than they have received heretofore.

Because of a deep preoccupation with the fragility of human existence, timepieces became very important symbols in Spanish Golden Age poetry. Certain themes became standard in the poetic canon. The best of these poems focus on the age-old paradoxes of the definition and nature of time. The very impossibility of defining time makes it a perfect point of departure for questioning man's position in a universe of unknowns, and since time is invisible and difficult to conceptualize, it must be represented symbolically, as by the timepiece or other objects that note the passage of time. The treatment of the clock in poetry traces a clear trajectory from Juan de Mena's initial curiosity through Quevedo's deep preoccupation to Torre y Sevil's fussy concern with niceties of decorative imagery. Undoubtedly one of the most important images in the poetry of "desengaño," the timepiece became a powerful symbol for a restless age, and the use of the image continued even after it had lost its initial significance.

Conclusion

The study of mechanical imagery in Spanish Baroque poetry reveals several important aspects of Golden Age poetry that have been previously overlooked. Mechanical imagery is found in all types of poetry, from the most traditional *romance* to the most baroque of *culterano* poems, and many poets at the beginning of the seventeenth century show an interest in it. The use of this type of imagery forms a parallel development with English poetry of the same period, and the recognition of its existence in Spain results in the discovery of a minor school of Spanish metaphysical poets—a fact completely ignored in previous Golden Age studies.

In addition, the study of this imagery reveals new facets in individual writers. As might be expected, Quevedo is the poet who extracts the most profound comparisons from the mechanical imagery. Lope de Vega shows the most interest in the observation of details, be it the imperceptible movement of the clock or the movement of iron filings in the presence of a magnet. It is difficult to imagine the busy poet and lover pausing to make such observations, and this aspect of his writing seems to contradict the traditional view of a hasty, uncritical writer. Even if the images were incorporated from other writers, they show an interest in minute observation that is not often associated with Lope. This aspect serves to complete the view of the Renaissance man, excelling as poet, soldier, lover and scholar.

Most of the devices treated in this study rely on an innate dualism. They are apparatus that consist of two parts or have two parts that function interdependently. The compass has two points, one of which is stationary and the other movable. The balance has two pans whose relationship is always inversely relative to the other. The navigational compass mysteriously always points to the north. Only the clock as a mechanical device does not involve an inherent dual nature. As an instrument, it serves to measure for man the passing of time, and thus to relate his existence to the invisible and barely perceptible metaphysical concept of time. Even though many of the metaphorical uses of the clock seem to point in other directions, nearly every example depends on an unspoken sense of the inevitable passage of time. The dualism of these instruments is employed as a linking device to place in a fixed relationship objects or concepts that cannot otherwise be considered as related. Much of the imagery relates the macrocosm to the microcosm, relying on the humblest of devices to delineate nearly inconceivable aspects of man's spiritual nature. Metaphysical poetry brought into play the paradoxes of man's existence in a world of flux governed by an immutable eternal godhead. The dual nature of the mechanical device served perfectly to show a relationship between these two worlds, be it paradoxical (balance), mechanical (geometer's compass), or hidden (navigational compass).

Ironically, the interest in mechanical devices, and a better understanding of physics and mathematics, would change man's understanding of the spiritual world and in many cases would lead to the negation of its existence altogether. But in the seventeenth century, an appreciation of the mechanical was only the first step in this direction, and was seen as lending support to the already existing knowledge of the cosmos. Humanist idealism was able to posit a syncretism and see a bit of

God's truth in all aspects of creation, from the pagan myths to the workings of the physical world.

The Baroque era exists at the end of the belief in the old order and the beginning of the new. In many respects it constitutes one last, almost desperate attempt to believe in or even reconstruct the carefully wrought medieval synthesis that produced the Christian cosmology. This explains in part the invention of a poetic of correspondences based on the phantasmagoric in which evident untruths were used to produce real spiritual truths. The welter of science and pseudo-science was transcended and writers arrived again at the long hallowed archetypes: the comfort of pure Platonic idealism, the perfection of the circle, the microcosm as image of the macrocosm. The exuberance and pomp barely served to mask the agonizing reality of the breakup of the old order, be it social, scientific, or philosophical, as the appearance of new ideas continually threatened and even encroached on the traditional havens of belief.

This study has shown that the scientific and technical were utilized to reinforce the old cosmological view. The secret forces of nature and the instability and destructiveness of time come to manifest themselves in concrete poetic imagery and, through their correspondences, point to ancient truths and reaffirm the old cosmology. Like so much of Baroque art, the new, in this case the geometrization of space and the new scientific attitudes, are incorporated into and actually serve as proofs of the existence of the old.